Ancient Texts and the Bible
Book 4 - Easy Reader Edition

In The Beginning...
From Israel to Egypt

Minister 2 Others

Ancient Texts and the Bible
Book 4

In The Beginning...
From Israel to Egypt

Easy Reader Edition

In The Beginning... From Israel to Egypt
ISBN 978-1-947751-22-4

Ancient texts compiled for this series:

The Bible
King James Version 1769

The Book of Enoch
An English translation by Dr. Laurence,
Archbishop of Cashel,
Formerly professor of Hebrew at Oxford, 1833

The Book of Jasher
Faithfully translated 1840
From the original Hebrew into English
Published by J.H. Parry & Company 1887

The Book of Jubilees
By R.H. Charles, Oxford: Clarendon Press, 1913

Ancient Texts and the Bible
series include:

Book 1: In The Beginning... From Adam to Noah
Book 2: In The Beginning... From Noah to Abraham
Book 3: In The Beginning... From Abraham to Israel
Book 4: In The Beginning... From Israel to Egypt
Book 5: In The Beginning... From Egypt to Goshen

Book 6: Israel... From Goshen to Sinai
Book 7: Israel... From Sinai to the Tabernacle
Book 8: Israel... Through the Book of Leviticus
Book 9: Israel... Through the Book of Numbers
Book 10: Israel... Through the Book of Joshua

Table of Contents:

Forward

The **Ancient Texts and the Bible** series synchronizes the manuscripts of Enoch, Jasher, and Jubilees into the Bible, making one complete storyline. The books are interwoven using the Torah as the backbone, and the extra-biblical texts as the fleshing out of that backbone.

The fourth book in the series contains Genesis 31-39, as well as the book of Jasher chapters 31-44, and the book of Jubilees chapters 29-39.

Though the language in the writings have been updated, replacing words like "*thou*" and "*thine*" with words like "*you*" and "*your*", the integrity of the verses remain.

The "*Easy Reader*" edition is for those who just want to read the storyline and enjoy the journey. The stop signs and complex formatting have been removed so one may merely focus upon the story being told.

The *Expanded Edition* of **Ancient Texts and the Bible** was created for the more studious reader. The various manuscripts have the following formatting applied to them in this edition:

the Bible - Regular

THE BOOK OF ENOCH - ALL CAPITALS

the Book of Jasher - Italics

the Book of Jubilees - Underlined

Where one of the extra-biblical texts reiterates the Bible, the phrase is then put in a **bold font**. Where two manuscripts overlap each other exclusive of the Bible, then both fonts are used. For instance, where Jasher and Jubilees intercept, the text is then formatted as *Italics and Underlined*.

The stop sign is another element to the *Expanded Edition* that is not seen in the *Easy Reader*. This image points to contradictions in the content. Printed versions also contain page numbers within the stop sign revealing the page where contradictory information is located, and vice versa. This information was not feasible to place in the e-book versions since the page numbers vary depending on the font size the reader chooses. Following, is an example from each edition:

Easy Reader Edition:

(Numbers 1:2) (Jasher 83:18...)
Take you the sum of all the heads of the congregation of the children of Israel, after their families, by the house of their fathers, with the number of their names, every male by their polls;

Expanded Edition:

(Numbers 1:2) (Jasher 83:18...)
Take you the sum of all *the heads of* the congregation of **the children of Israel,** after their families, by the house of their fathers, with the number of their names, **every male** by their polls;

Whichever you choose, may you ***Enjoy the Journey***!

Prologue

(Jasher 31:34) (Jubilees 28:30)
And Jacob obtained riches and honor and possessions by means of these transactions with the sons of men; And Laban and the children of Laban envied him of this honor, and Laban took back his sheep from him, and he observed him with evil intent.

Genesis: Chapter Thirty-One

(Genesis 31:1) (Jasher 31:35)

And in the course of time, he heard the words of Laban's sons, saying, Jacob has taken away all that was our father's; and of that which was our father's, he has gotten all this glory.

(Genesis 31:2) (Jasher 31:36)

And Jacob beheld the countenance of Laban and of his children, and, behold, it was not toward him in those days as it had been before.

(Jubilees 29:1)

And it came to pass when Rachel had borne Joseph, that Laban went to shear his sheep; for they were distant from him a three days' journey.

(Genesis 31:3) (Jasher 31:37)

And the Lord appeared to Jacob at the expiration of the six years. And the LORD said to Jacob, Arise, go forth out of this land, and return to the land of your birthplace, to your fathers, and to your kindred; and I will be with you.

(Genesis 31:4) (Jubilees 29:2)

And Jacob saw that Laban was going to shear his sheep, and Jacob sent and called Rachel and Leah to the field to his flock, and spoke kindly to them that they should come with him to the land of Canaan.

(Genesis 31:5)

And said to them, I see your father's countenance, that it is not toward me as before; but the God of my father has been with me.

(Genesis 31:6)

And you know that with all my power I have served your father.

(Genesis 31:7)

And your father has deceived me, and changed my wages ten times; but God suffered him not to hurt me.

(Genesis 31:8)

If he said thus, The speckled shall be your wages; then all the cattle bore speckled: and if he said thus, The ringstraked shall be your hire; then bore all the cattle ringstraked.

(Genesis 31:9)

Thus, God has taken away the cattle of your father, and given them to me.

(Genesis 31:10)

And it came to pass at the time that the cattle conceived, that I lifted up my eyes, and saw in a dream, and, behold, the rams which leaped on the cattle were ringstraked, speckled, and grizzled.

(Genesis 31:11) (Jubilees 29:3...)

For he told them how he had seen everything in a dream, even all that He had spoken to him that he should return to his father's house. And the angel of God spoke to me in a dream, saying, Jacob: And I said, Here am I.

(Genesis 31:12)

And he said, Lift up now your eyes, and see, all the rams which leap on the cattle are ringstraked, speckled, and grizzled: for I have seen all that Laban does to you.

(Genesis 31:13)

I am the God of Bethel, where you anointed the pillar, and where you vowed a vow to me: now arise, get you out from this land, and return to the land of your kindred.

(Genesis 31:14) (...Jubilees 29:3)

And Rachel and Leah answered and they said to him: To every place where you go we will go with you. Is there yet any portion or inheritance for us in our father's house?

(Genesis 31:15)

Are we not counted of him strangers? For he has sold us, and has quite devoured also our money.

(Genesis 31:16)

For all the riches which God has taken from our father, that is ours, and our children's: now then, whatsoever God has said to you, do.

(Genesis 31:17) (Jasher 31:38...) (Jubilees 29:4...)

And Jacob blessed the God of Isaac his father, and the God of Abraham his father's father. Then Jacob rose up at that time, and he set his sons and his wives and all belonging to him on camels;

(Genesis 31:18) (...Jasher 31:38)

And he carried away all his cattle, and all his goods which he had gotten, the cattle of his getting, which he had gotten in Padanaram, to go to Isaac his father in the land of Canaan.

(Genesis 31:19) (Jasher 31:39..., 40)

And Laban went to shear his sheep: and Rachel had stolen the images that were her father's and she took them and she concealed them upon the camel upon which she sat, and she went on.

(Genesis 31:20) (...Jasher 31:39) (...Jubilees 29:4)

And Jacob crossed the river, and came to the land of Gilead. Jacob stole away unawares to Laban the Syrian, in that he did not tell him that he fled.

(Genesis 31:21)

So he fled with all that he had; and he rose up, and passed over the river, and set his face toward the Mount Gilead.

~ ~ ~

(Jasher 31:41)

And this is the manner of the images; in taking a man who is the first born and slaying him and taking the hair off his head, and taking salt and salting the head and anointing it in oil, then taking a small tablet of copper or a tablet of gold and writing the name upon it, and placing the tablet under his tongue, and taking the head with the tablet under the tongue and putting it in the house, and lighting up lights before it and bowing down to it.

(Jasher 31:42)

And at the time when they bow down to it, it speaks to them in all matters that they ask of it, through the power of the name which is written in it.

(Jasher 31:43)
And some make them in the figures of men, of gold and silver, and go to them in times known to them, and the figures receive the influence of the stars, and tell them future things, and in this manner were the images which Rachel stole from her father.

(Jasher 31:44)
And Rachel stole these images which were her father's, in order that Laban might not know through them where Jacob had gone.

(Genesis 31:22) (Jasher 31:45)
And Laban came home and he asked concerning Jacob and his household, and he was not to be found, and Laban sought his images to know where Jacob had gone, and could not find them, and he went to some other images, and he inquired of them and it was told Laban on the third day that Jacob had fled from him to go to his father's, to the land of Canaan.

(Genesis 31:23) (Jasher 31:46) (Jubilees 29:5)
And in the seventh year of the fourth week Jacob turned (his face) toward Gilead in the first month, on the twenty-first thereof. And Laban then rose up and he took his brothers and all his servants with him, and he went forth and pursued after him seven days' journey; and they overtook him in the mount Gilead in the third month, on the thirteenth thereof.

(Genesis 31:24) (Jubilees 29:6...)
And the Lord God did not suffer him to injure Jacob; for He came and appeared to Laban the Syrian in a dream by night, and said to him, Take heed that you do not speak Jacob either good or bad.

(Genesis 31:25)

Then Laban overtook Jacob. Now Jacob had pitched his tent in the mount: and Laban with his brothers pitched in the mount of Gilead.

(Genesis 31:26) (Jasher 31:47) (...Jubilees 29:6)

And Laban said to Jacob, What have you done, that you have stolen away unawares to me and deceive me, and carried away my daughters and their children, as captives taken with the sword?

(Genesis 31:27) (Jasher 31:48...)

Why did you flee away secretly, and steal away from me; and did not tell me, that I might have sent you away with mirth, and with songs, with timbrel, and with harp?

(Genesis 31:28) (...Jasher 31:48)

And have not suffered me to kiss my sons and my daughters? And you stole my gods and went away; you have now done foolishly in so doing.

(Genesis 31:29)

It is in the power of my hand to do you hurt: but the God of your father spoke to me last night, saying, Take heed that you speak not to Jacob either good or bad.

(Genesis 31:30)

And now, though you have certainly gone, because you so long for your father's house, yet why have you stolen my gods?

(Genesis 31:31) (Jasher 31:49...)

And Jacob answered and said to Laban, Because I was afraid: for I said, Peradventure you would take by force your daughters from me.

(Genesis 31:32) (...Jasher 31:49)
With whomsoever you find your gods, let him not live: before our brothers, discern what is yours with me, and take it to you. For Jacob did not know that Rachel had stolen them.

(Genesis 31:33) (Jasher 31:50...)
And Laban went into Jacob's tent, and searched for the images and he examined in all Jacob's tents and furniture and into Leah's tent, and into the two maidservants' tents; but he found them not. Then went he out of Leah's tent, and entered into Rachel's tent.

(Genesis 31:34) (...Jasher 31:50)
Now Rachel had taken the images, and put them in the camel's furniture, and sat on them. And Laban searched all the tent, but did not find them.

(Genesis 31:35)
And she said to her father, Let it not displease my lord that I cannot rise up before you; for the custom of women is on me. And he searched, but did not find the images.

(Genesis 31:36)
And Jacob was furious, and strove with Laban: and Jacob answered and said to Laban, What is my trespass? What is my sin, that you have so hotly pursued after me?

(Genesis 31:37)
Whereas you have searched all my stuff, what have you found of all your household stuff? Set it here before my brothers and your brothers, that they may judge between us both.

(Genesis 31:38)
This twenty years have I been with you; your ewes and your

she goats have not cast their young, and the rams of your flock I have not eaten.

(Genesis 31:39)
That which was torn of beasts I brought not to you; I bore the loss of it; of my hand you required it, whether stolen by day, or stolen by night.

(Genesis 31:40)
Thus, I was; in the day the drought consumed me, and the frost by night; and my sleep departed from my eyes.

(Genesis 31:41)
Thus, have I been twenty years in your house; I served you fourteen years for your two daughters, and six years for your cattle: and you have changed my wages ten times.

(Genesis 31:42)
Except the God of my father, the God of Abraham, and the fear of Isaac, had been with me, surely you would have sent me away now empty. God has seen my affliction and the labor of my hands, and rebuked you last night.

(Genesis 31:43)
And Laban answered and said to Jacob, These daughters are my daughters, and these children are my children, and these cattle are my cattle, and all that you see is mine: and what can I do this day to these my daughters, or to their children which they have born?

(Genesis 31:44) (Jasher 31:51...)
And Laban said to Jacob, Now therefore, come, let us make a covenant together, I and you; and let it be for a witness between me and you.

(Genesis 31:45)
And Jacob took a stone, and set it up for a pillar.

(Genesis 31:46) (Jasher 31:52...)
And Jacob said to his brothers, Gather stones; and they took stones, and made a heap: and they ate there on the heap.

(Genesis 31:47)
And Laban called it Jegarsahadutha: but Jacob called it Galeed.

(Genesis 31:48) (...Jasher 31:52)
And Laban said, This heap is a witness between me and you this day. Therefore, was the name of it called Galeed;

(Genesis 31:49)
And Mizpah; for he said, The LORD watch between me and you, when we are absent one from another.

(Genesis 31:50) (...Jasher 31:51)
If you shall afflict my daughters, or if you shall take other wives beside my daughters, no man is with us; see, God is witness between me and you in this matter.

(Genesis 31:51)
And Laban said to Jacob, Behold this heap, and behold this pillar, which I have cast between me and you;

(Genesis 31:52)
This heap be witness, and this pillar be witness, that I will not pass over this heap to you, and that you shall not pass over this heap and this pillar to me, for harm.

(Genesis 31:53)
The God of Abraham, and the God of Nahor, the God of their father, judge between us. And Jacob swore by the fear of his father Isaac.

(Jubilees 29:7)
And on the fifteenth of those days Jacob made a feast for Laban, and for all who came with him, and Jacob swore to Laban that day, and Laban also to Jacob, that neither should cross the mountain of Gilead to the other with evil purpose.

(Jubilees 29:8)
And he made there a heap for a witness; wherefore the name of that place is called: 'The Heap of Witness,' after this heap.

(Jubilees 29:9)
But before they used to call the land of Gilead the land of the Rephaim; for it was the land of the Rephaim, and the Rephaim were born there, giants whose height was ten, nine, eight down to seven cubits.

(Jubilees 29:10)
And their habitation was from the land of the children of Ammon to Mount Hermon, and the seats of their kingdom were Karnaim and Ashtaroth, and Edrei, and Misur, and Beon.

(Jubilees 29:11)
And the Lord destroyed them because of the evil of their deeds; for they were very malignant, and the Amorites dwelt in their stead, wicked and sinful, and there is no people to-day which has wrought to the full all their sins, and they have no longer length of life on the earth.

(Genesis 31:54) (Jasher 31:53...)
Then Jacob and Laban offered sacrifice on the mountain, and called his brothers to eat bread: and they ate bread there by the heap, and tarried all night in the mountain.

(Genesis 31:55) (...Jasher 31:53) (Jubilees 29:12)
And early in the morning Laban rose up, and he wept with his daughters and kissed his sons and his daughters, and blessed them. And Jacob sent away Laban and Laban departed, and returned to his place in Mesopotamia, the land of the East, and Jacob returned to the land of Gilead.

(Jasher 31:54)
And he hastened and sent off his son Beor, who was seventeen years old, with Abichorof the son of Uz, the son of Nahor, and with them were ten men.

(Jasher 31:55)
And they hastened and went and passed on the road before Jacob, and they came by another road to the land of Seir.

(Jasher 31:56)
And they came to Esau and said to him, Thus says your brother and relative, your mother's brother Laban, the son of Bethuel, saying,

(Jasher 31:57)
Have you heard what Jacob your brother has done to me, who first came to me naked and bare, and I went to meet him, and brought him to my house with honor, and I made him great, and I gave him my two daughters for wives and also two of my maids.

(Jasher 31:58)
And God blessed him on my account, and he increased abundantly, and had sons, daughters and maid servants.

(Jasher 31:59)
He has also an immense stock of flocks and herds, camels and donkeys, also silver and gold in abundance; and when he saw that his wealth increased, he left me while I went to shear my sheep, and he rose up and fled in secrecy.

(Jasher 31:60)
And he lifted his wives and children upon camels, and he led away all his cattle and property which he acquired in my land, and he lifted up his countenance to go to his father Isaac, to the land of Canaan.

(Jasher 31:61)
And he did not suffer me to kiss my daughters and their children, and he led my daughters as captives taken by the sword, and he also stole my gods and he fled.

(Jasher 31:62)
And now I have left him in the mountain of the brook of Jabuk, him and all belonging to him; he lacks nothing.

(Jasher 31:63)
If it be your wish to go to him, go then and there will you find him, and you can do to him as your soul desires; and Laban's messengers came and told Esau all these things.

(Jasher 31:64)
And Esau heard all the words of Laban's messengers, and his anger was greatly kindled against Jacob, and he remembered his hatred, and his anger burned within him.

(Jasher 31:65)
And Esau hastened and took his children and servants and the souls of his household, being sixty men, and he went and assembled all the children of Seir the Horite and their people, being three hundred and forty men, and took all this number of four hundred men with drawn swords, and he went to Jacob to smite him.

(Jasher 31:66)
And Esau divided this number into several parts, and he took the sixty men of his children and servants and the souls of his household as one head, and gave them in care of Eliphaz his eldest son.

(Jasher 31:67)
And the remaining heads he gave to the care of the six sons of Seir the Horite, and he placed every man over his generations and children.

(Jasher 31:68)
And the whole of this camp went as it was, and Esau went among them toward Jacob, and he conducted them with speed.

(Jasher 31:69)
And Laban's messengers departed from Esau and went to the land of Canaan, and they came to the house of Rebecca the mother of Jacob and Esau.

(Jasher 31:70)
And they told her saying, Behold your son Esau has gone against his brother Jacob with four hundred men, for he heard that he was coming, and he is gone to make war with him, and to smite him and to take all that he has.

(Jasher 31:71)
And Rebecca hastened and sent seventy-two men from the servants of Isaac to meet Jacob on the road; for she said, Peradventure, Esau may make war in the road when he meets him.

Genesis: Chapter Thirty-Two

(Genesis 32:1) (Jasher 31:72...)

And Jacob went on his way. And these messengers went on the road to meet Jacob, and the angels of God, messengers sent from Rebecca, met him in the road of the brook on the opposite side of the brook Jabuk.

(Genesis 32:2) (...Jasher 31:72)

And when Jacob saw them, he said, This is God's host: This camp is destined to me from God, and he called the name of that place Mahanaim.

(Jasher 31:73)

And Jacob knew all his father's people, and he kissed them and embraced them and came with them, and Jacob asked them concerning his father and mother, and they said, They were well.

(Jasher 31:74)

And these messengers said to Jacob, Rebecca your mother has sent us to you, saying, I have heard, my son, that your brother Esau has gone forth against you on the road with men from the children of Seir the Horite.

(Jasher 31:75)

And therefore, my son, hearken to my voice and see with your counsel what you will do, and when he comes up to you, supplicate him, and do not speak rashly to him, and give him a present from what you possess, and from what God has favored you with.

(Jasher 31:76)
And when he asks you concerning your affairs, conceal nothing from him, perhaps he may turn from his anger against you and you will thereby save your soul, you and all belonging to you, for it is your duty to honor him, for he is your elder brother.

(Jasher 31:77)
And when Jacob heard the words of his mother which the messengers had spoken to him, Jacob lifted up his voice and wept bitterly, and did as his mother then commanded him.

(Genesis 32:3) (Jasher 32:1)
And at that time Jacob sent messengers before him to Esau his brother to the land of Seir, the country of Edom and he spoke to him words of supplication.

(Genesis 32:4) (Jasher 32:2, 3)
And he commanded them, saying, Thus you shall speak to my lord Esau; Your servant Jacob says thus, Let not my lord imagine that my father's blessing with which he blessed me has proved beneficial to me. I have sojourned these twenty years with Laban, and stayed there until now: and he deceived me and changed my wages ten times, as it has all been already told to my lord.

(Jasher 32:4)
And I served him in his house very laboriously, and God afterward saw my affliction, my labor and the work of my hands, and he caused me to find grace and favor in his sight.

(Genesis 32:5) (Jasher 32:5, 6)
And I afterward through God's great mercy and kindness have oxen, and donkeys, flocks, and men servants, and women

servants. And now I am coming to my land and my home to my father and mother, who are in the land of Canaan; and I have sent to tell my lord all this, that I may find grace in your sight so that you may not imagine that I have of myself obtained wealth, or that the blessing with which my father blessed me has benefited me.

(Jasher 32:7)
And those messengers went to Esau, and found him on the borders of the land of Edom going toward Jacob, and four hundred men of the children of Seir the Horite were standing with drawn swords.

(Jasher 32:8)
And the messengers of Jacob told Esau all the words that Jacob had spoken to them concerning Esau.

(Jasher 32:9)
And Esau answered them with pride and contempt, and said to them, Surely, I have heard and truly it has been told to me what Jacob has done to Laban, who exalted him in his house and gave him his daughters for wives, and he begot sons and daughters, and abundantly increased in wealth and riches in Laban's house through his means.

(Jasher 32:10)
And when he saw that his wealth was abundant and his riches great he fled with all belonging to him, from Laban's house, and he led Laban's daughters away from the face of their father, as captives taken by the sword without telling him of it.

(Jasher 32:11)
And not only to Laban has Jacob done thus but also to me has

he done so and has twice supplanted me, and shall I be silent?

(Jasher 32:12)
Now therefore I have this day come with my camps to meet him, and I will do to him according to the desire of my heart.

(Genesis 32:6) (Jasher 32:13)
And the messengers returned and came to Jacob, and spoke to him saying, We came to your brother Esau, and we told him all your words, and thus has he answered us, and also he comes to meet you, and four hundred men with him.

(Jasher 32:14)
Now then know and see what you shall do, and pray before God to deliver you from him.

(Genesis 32:7...) (Jasher 32:15)
And when he heard the words of his brother which he had spoken to the messengers of Jacob, then Jacob was greatly afraid and he was distressed:

(...Genesis 32:7) (Jasher 32:24)
And he divided the people that was with him, and the flocks, and herds, and the camels, into two bands; and he gave the half to the care of Damesek, the son of Eliezer, Abraham's servant, for a camp, with his children, and the other half he gave to the care of his brother Elianus the son of Eliezer, to be for a camp with his children.

(Genesis 32:8) (Jasher 32:25)
And he commanded them and said, Keep yourselves at a distance with your camps, and do not come too near each other, and if Esau come to the one company, and smite it,

then the other company at a distance from it which is left shall escape him.

(Jasher 32:26...)
And Jacob tarried there that night, and during the whole night he gave his servants instructions concerning the forces and his children.

(Genesis 32:9...) (Jasher 32:16)
And Jacob prayed to the Lord his God, and he said, O Lord God of my father Abraham and God of my father Isaac, the LORD Who said to me, when I went away from my father's house, saying,

(Jasher 32:17)
I am the Lord God of your father Abraham and the God of Isaac, to you do I give this land and your seed after you, and I will make your seed as the stars of heaven, and you shall spread forth to the four sides of heaven, and in you and in your seed shall all the families of the earth be blessed.

(Jasher 32:18)
And you established your words, and gave to me riches and children and cattle, as the utmost wishes of my heart you gave to your servant; you gave to me all that I asked from you, so that I lacked nothing.

(...Genesis 32:9) (Jasher 32:19)
And afterward you said to me, Return to your country, and to your kindred, and to your birth place and I will deal well with you:

(Genesis 32:10) (Jasher 32:23...)
I am not worthy of the least of all the mercies, and of all the

truth, which You have showed to Your servant; for with my staff I passed over this Jordan; and now I am become two bands. For I know that through kindness and mercy I have acquired this wealth;

(Jasher 32:20...)
And now that I have come, and you delivered me from Laban, shall I fall in the hands of Esau?

(Jasher 32:22)
If there is no righteousness in me, do it for the sake of Abraham and my father Isaac.

(Genesis 32:11) (...Jasher 32:20, 21)
Now therefore, O Lord God, deliver me, I pray, from the hand of my brother, from the hand of Esau: for I greatly fear him, lest he comes and smite me, and the mother with the children.

(Genesis 32:12) (...Jasher 32:23)
And You said, I will surely do you good, and make your seed as the sand of the sea, which cannot be numbered for multitude, now therefore I beseech you to deliver me this day with your kindness and answer me.

(...Jasher 32:24...)
And Jacob ceased praying to the Lord.

(Jasher 32:27)
And the Lord heard the prayer of Jacob on that day, and the Lord then delivered Jacob from the hands of his brother Esau.

(Jasher 32:28)
And the Lord sent three angels of the angels of heaven, and they went before Esau and came to him.

(Jasher 32:29)
And these angels appeared to Esau and his people as two thousand men, riding upon horses furnished with all sorts of war instruments, and they appeared in the sight of Esau and all his men to be divided into four camps, with four chiefs to them.

(Jasher 32:30)
And one camp went on and they found Esau coming with four hundred men toward his brother Jacob, and this camp ran toward Esau and his people and terrified them, and Esau fell off the horse in alarm, and all his men separated from him in that place, for they were greatly afraid.

(Jasher 32:31)
And the whole of the camp shouted after them when they fled from Esau, and all the warlike men answered, saying,

(Jasher 32:32)
Surely, we are the servants of Jacob, who is the servant of God, and who then can stand against us? And Esau said to them, O then, my lord and brother Jacob is your lord, whom I have not seen for these twenty years, and now that I have this day come to see him, do you treat me in this manner?

(Jasher 32:33)
And the angels answered him saying, As the Lord lives, were not Jacob of whom you speak your brother, we had not let one remaining from you and your people, but only on account of Jacob we will do nothing to them.

(Jasher 32:34)
And this camp passed from Esau and his men and it went away, and Esau and his men had gone from them about a

league when the second camp came toward him with all sorts of weapons, and they also did to Esau and his men as the first camp had done to them.

(Jasher 32:35)
And when they had left it to go on, behold the third camp came toward him and they were all terrified, and Esau fell off the horse, and the whole camp cried out, and said, Surely, we are the servants of Jacob, who is the servant of God, and who can stand against us?

(Jasher 32:36)
And Esau again answered them saying, O then, Jacob my lord and your lord is my brother, and for twenty years I have not seen his countenance and hearing this day that he was coming, I went this day to meet him, and do you treat me in this manner?

(Jasher 32:37)
And they answered him, and said to him, As the Lord lives, if Jacob was not your brother as you said, we would have not left a remnant from you and your men, but on account of Jacob of whom you speak being your brother, we will not meddle with you or your men.

(Jasher 32:38)
And the third camp also passed from them, and he still continued his road with his men toward Jacob, when the fourth camp came toward him, and they also did to him and his men as the others had done.

(Jasher 32:39)
And when Esau beheld the evil which the four angels had done to him and to his men, he became greatly afraid of his

brother Jacob, and he went to meet him in peace.

(Jasher 32:40)
And Esau concealed his hatred against Jacob, because he was afraid of his life on account of his brother Jacob, and because he imagined that the four camps that he had lighted upon were Jacob's servants.

(Genesis 32:13) (Jasher 32:41)
And Jacob lodged there that same night with his servants in their camps, and he resolved with his servants to give to Esau a present from all that he had with him, and from all his property; and Jacob rose up in the morning, he and his men, and they took from among the cattle of that which came to his hand a present for Esau his brother;

(Genesis 32:14) (Jasher 32:42...)
And this is the amount of the present which Jacob chose from his flock to give to his brother Esau: and he selected two hundred she goats, and twenty he goats, two hundred ewes, and twenty rams, two hundred and forty head from the flocks.

(Genesis 32:15) (...Jasher 32:42)
And he selected thirty milk camels with their colts, forty cows, and ten bulls (fifty kine), twenty she donkeys, and ten foals (thirty donkeys).

(Genesis 32:16) (Jasher 32:43, 44...)
And he put them all in ten droves, and he placed each sort by itself. And he delivered them into the hand of ten of his servants, every drove by themselves. And he commanded them, and said to his servants, Pass over before me, Keep yourselves at a distance from each other, and put a space between drove and drove.

(Genesis 32:17) (...Jasher 32:44...)

And he commanded the foremost, saying, When Esau my brother and those who are with him meets you, and asks you, saying, Whose are you? And where are you going? And whose are these before you?

(Genesis 32:18) (...Jasher 32:44)

Then you shall say to them, These are your servant Jacob's; We are the servants of Jacob. It is a present sent to my lord Esau: we come to meet Esau in peace; and, behold, Jacob comes also, he is behind us.

(Jasher 32:45)

And that which is before us is a present sent from Jacob to his brother Esau

(Genesis 32:19)

And so he commanded the second, and the third, and all that followed the droves, saying, On this manner shall you speak to Esau, when you find him.

(Genesis 32:20) (Jasher 32:46)

And if they shall say to you, Why does he delay behind you, from coming to meet his brother and to see his face, then you shall say moreover to them, Surely he comes joyfully behind us to meet his brother. Behold, your servant Jacob is behind us. For he said, I will appease him with the present that goes before me to him, and afterward I will see his face; peradventure he will accept of me.

(Genesis 32:21) (Jasher 32:47...)

So the whole present passed on in the hands of his servants, and went over before him on that day: and he lodged that night in the company by the border of the brook of Jabuk.

(Genesis 32:22) (...Jasher 32:47)

And he rose up the midst of that night, and took his two wives, and his two women servants, and his eleven sons, and all belonging to him, and he that night passed over the ford Jabbok.

(Genesis 32:23) (Jasher 32:48...)

And he took them, and sent them over the brook, and sent over that he had.

(Genesis 32:24) (...Jasher 32:48...)

And Jacob was left alone; and there a man met him, and he wrestled with him that night until the breaking of the day.

(Genesis 32:25) (...Jasher 32:48)

And when he saw that He prevailed not against him, He touched the hollow of his thigh; and the hollow of Jacob's thigh was out of joint, as He wrestled with him.

(Genesis 32:26)

And He said, Let me go, for the day breaks. And he said, I will not let you go, except you bless me.

(Genesis 32:27)

And He said to him, What is your name? And he said, Jacob.

(Genesis 32:28)

And He said, Your name shall be called no more Jacob, but Israel: for as a prince have you power with God and with men, and have prevailed.

(Genesis 32:29) (Jasher 32:49...)

And Jacob asked Him, and said, Tell me, I pray, your name. And He said, Why is it that you ask after my name? And at the break of day the man left Jacob there, and He blessed him there and went away.

(Genesis 32:30)

And Jacob called the name of the place Peniel: for I have seen God face to face, and my life is preserved.

(Genesis 32:31) (...Jasher 32:49, 50)

And as he passed over the brook at Penuel, at the break of day. And the sun rose on him, when he had passed the brook, and he came up to the place of his cattle and children. And he halted on his thigh.

(Genesis 32:32)

Therefore, the children of Israel eat not of the sinew which shrank, which is on the hollow of the thigh, to this day: because he touched the hollow of Jacob's thigh in the sinew that shrank.

Genesis: Chapter Thirty-Three

(Jubilees 29:13...)
And he passed over the Jabbok in the ninth month, on the eleventh thereof.

(Jasher 32:51)
And they went on till midday, and while they were going the present was passing on before them.

(Genesis 33:1) (Jasher 32:52, 53)
And Jacob lifted up his eyes, and looked, and, behold, Esau at a distance, came, and with him many men, about four hundred men. And Jacob was greatly afraid of his brother. And he hastened and divided the children to Leah, and to Rachel, and to the two handmaids. And his daughter Dinah he put in a chest, and delivered her into the hands of his servants.

(Genesis 33:2)
And he put the handmaids and their children foremost, and Leah and her children after, and Rachel and Joseph hindermost.

(Genesis 33:3) (Jasher 32:54)
And he passed over before them, to meet his brother, and bowed himself to the ground seven times, until he came near to his brother. And God caused Jacob to find grace and favor in the sight of Esau and his men, for God had heard the prayer of Jacob.

(Jasher 32:55)
And the fear of Jacob and his terror fell upon his brother Esau, for Esau was greatly afraid of Jacob for what the angels of God had done to Esau, and Esau's anger against Jacob was turned into kindness.

(Genesis 33:4) (Jasher 32:56)

And when Esau saw Jacob running toward him, he also ran to meet him, and embraced him, and fell on his neck, and kissed him: and they wept.

(Jasher 32:57)
And God put fear and kindness toward Jacob in the hearts of the men that came with Esau, and they also kissed Jacob and embraced him.

(Jasher 32:58)
And also Eliphaz, the son of Esau, with his four brothers, sons of Esau, wept with Jacob, and they kissed him and embraced him, for the fear of Jacob had fallen upon them all.

(Genesis 33:5) (Jasher 32:59, 60)

And Esau lifted up his eyes, and saw the women and their offspring, the children of Jacob, walking behind Jacob and bowing along the road to Esau. And Esau said to Jacob, Who are those with you, my brother? Are they your children or your servants? And Jacob answered Esau and said, They are the children which God has graciously given your servant.

(Genesis 33:6)

Then the handmaidens came near, they and their children, and they bowed themselves.

(Genesis 33:7)
And Leah also with her children came near, and bowed themselves: and after came Joseph near and Rachel, and they bowed themselves.

(Genesis 33:8) (Jasher 32:61)
And while Jacob was speaking to Esau and his men, Esau beheld the whole camp, and he said to Jacob, Where did you get the whole of the camp that I met last night? What do you mean by all this drove which I met? And Jacob said, These are to find grace in the sight of my lord, it is that which God graciously gave to your servant.

(Genesis 33:9) (Jasher 32:62)
And the present came before Esau, and Jacob pressed Esau, saying, Take I pray you the present that I have brought to my lord. And Esau said, Wherefore is this my purpose? I have enough, my brother; keep what you have for yourself.

(Jasher 32:63)
And Jacob said, It is incumbent upon me to give all this, since I have seen your face, that you still live in peace.

(Genesis 33:10) (Jasher 32:64)
And Esau refused to take the present, and Jacob said to him, Nay, I pray, if now I have found grace in your sight, then receive my present at my hand: for therefore I have seen your face, as though I had seen the face of God, and you were pleased with me.

(Genesis 33:11) (Jasher 32:65)
Take, I pray, my blessing that is brought to you; because God has dealt graciously with me, and because I have enough. And he urged him, and Esau took the present, and Jacob also gave

to Esau silver and gold and bdellium, for he pressed him so much that he took it.

(Jasher 32:66)
And Esau divided the cattle that were in the camp, and he gave the half to the men who had come with him, for they had come on hire, and the other half he delivered to the hands of his children.

(Jasher 32:67...)
And the silver and gold and bdellium he gave in the hands of Eliphaz his eldest son.

(Genesis 33:12) (...Jasher 32:67)
And Esau said to Jacob, Let us remain with you, and take our journey, and let us go, and I will go before you and we will go slowly along with you until you come to my place with me, that we may dwell there together.

(Genesis 33:13) (Jasher 32:68)
And Jacob answered his brother and he said to him, I would do as my lord speaks to me, but my lord knows that the children are tender, and the flocks and herds with young are with me go but slowly, and if men should overdrive them one day and they went swiftly, all the flock will die for you know their burdens and their fatigue.

(Genesis 33:14) (Jasher 32:69)
Therefore, let my lord, I pray, pass over before his servant: and I will lead on softly, according as the cattle that go before me and the children be able to endure, until I come to my lord to Seir.

(Genesis 33:15) (Jasher 32:70)
And Esau said to Jacob, Let me now leave with you some of the folk that are with me to take care of you in the road, and to bear your fatigue and burden. And he said, What need is it? Let me find grace in the sight of my lord.

(Jasher 32:71)
Behold I will come to you to Seir to dwell there together as you have spoken, go you then with your people for I will follow you.

(Jasher 32:72)
And Jacob said this to Esau in order to remove Esau and his men from him, so that Jacob might afterward go to his father's house to the land of Canaan.

(Genesis 33:16) (Jasher 32:73) (...Jubilees 29:13)
And Esau hearkened to the voice of Jacob. So Esau his brother, came to him, and he was reconciled to him, and departed from him and returned that day with the four hundred men that were with him on his way to the land of Seir, but Jacob and all belonging to him went that day as far as the extremity of the land of Canaan in its borders, and Jacob remained there some time and dwelt in tents.

(Jubilees 29:14)
And in the first year of the fifth week in this jubilee, he crossed the Jordan, and dwelt beyond the Jordan, and he pastured his sheep from the sea of the heap to Bethshan, and to Dothan and to the forest of Akrabbim.

(Jubilees 29:15)
And he sent to his father Isaac of all his substance, clothing,

and food, and meat, and drink, and milk, and butter, and cheese, and some dates of the valley.

(Jubilees 29:16)
And to his mother Rebecca also four times a year, between the times of the months, between ploughing and reaping, and between autumn and the rain, and between winter and spring, to the tower of Abraham.

(Jubilees 29:17)
For Isaac had returned from the Well of the Oath and gone up to the tower of his father Abraham, and he dwelt there apart from his son Esau.

(Jubilees 29:18)
For in the days when Jacob went to Mesopotamia, Esau took to himself a wife Mahalath, the daughter of Ishmael, and he gathered together all the flocks of his father and his wives, and went up and dwelt on Mount Seir, and left Isaac his father at the Well of the Oath alone.

(Jubilees 29:19)
And Isaac went up from the Well of the Oath and dwelt in the tower of Abraham his father on the mountains of Hebron,

(Jubilees 29:20)
And there Jacob sent all that he sent to his father and his mother from time to time, all they needed, and they blessed Jacob with all their heart and with all their soul.

(Genesis 33:17) (Jasher 33:3)
And Jacob journeyed to Succoth, and built him a house, and he pitched his tent there, and made booths for his cattle: therefore, the name of the place he called Succoth.

(Genesis 33:18) (Jasher 33:1) (Jubilees 30:1)

And in some time after, in the first year of the sixth week, Jacob went away from the borders of the land, and he came to the land of Shalem, that is to the east of the city of Shechem, which is in the land of Canaan, when he came from Padanaram; and pitched his tent and rested before the city in peace, in the fourth month.

(Genesis 33:19) (Jasher 33:2)

And he bought a parcel of a field which was there, where he had spread his tent, at the hand of the people of the land, the children of Hamor, Shechem's father, for a hundred pieces of money, five shekels.

(Genesis 33:20)

And he erected there an altar, and called it El Elohe Israel.

(Jasher 33:4)

And Jacob remained in Succoth a year and six months.

Genesis: Chapter Thirty Four

(Jasher 33:5)
At that time, some of the women of the inhabitants of the land went to the city of Shechem to dance and rejoice with the daughters of the people of the city, and when they went forth then Rachel and Leah the wives of Jacob with their families also went to behold the rejoicing of the daughters of the city.

(Genesis 34:1) (Jasher 33:6)
And Dinah the daughter of Leah, which she bore to Jacob, also went along with them out to see the daughters of the city of the land. And they remained there before these daughters while all the people of the city were standing by them to behold their rejoicings, and all the great people of the city were there.

(Genesis 34:2...) (Jasher 33:7, 8)
And when Shechem the son of Hamor the Hivite, prince of the country, was also standing there to see them. And Shechem beheld Dinah the daughter of Jacob sitting with her mother before the daughters of the city, and the damsel pleased him greatly, and he there asked his friends and his people, saying, Whose daughter is that sitting among the women, whom I do not know in this city?

(Jasher 33:9)
And they said to him, Surely this is the daughter of Jacob the son of Isaac the Hebrew, who has dwelt in this city for some time, and when it was reported that the daughters of the land were going forth to rejoice she went with her mother and maid servants to sit among them as you see.

(Jasher 33:10)
And Shechem beheld Dinah the daughter of Jacob, and when he looked at her his soul became fixed upon Dinah.

(...Genesis 34:2) (Jasher 33:11...) (Jubilees 30:2)
And he sent and he took her by force, and they carried off Dinah, the daughter of Jacob, and Dinah came to the house of Shechem, the son of Hamor, the Hivite, the prince of the land, and he seized her forcibly and lay with her, and defiled her, and she was a little girl, a child of twelve years.

(Genesis 34:3) (...Jasher 33:11)
And his soul clave to Dinah the daughter of Jacob, and he loved the damsel exceedingly, and spoke kindly to the damsel and placed her in his house.

(Genesis 34:4) (Jasher 33:16...) (Jubilees 30:3...)
And Shechem sent three of his friends to his father Hamor, the son of Chiddekem, the son of Pered, saying, Get me this damsel to wife.

(Jasher 33:17)
And Hamor the son of Chiddekem the Hivite came to the house of Shechem his son, and he sat before him, and Hamor said to his son, Shechem, Is there then no woman among the daughters of your people that you will take an Hebrew woman who is not of your people?

(Jasher 33:18)
And Shechem said to him, Her only must you get for me, for she is delightful in my sight; and Hamor did according to the word of his son, for he was greatly beloved by him

(Genesis 34:5...) (Jasher 33:12)

And they came and told the thing to Jacob, and when Jacob heard that Shechem had defiled Dinah his daughter: Jacob sent twelve of his servants to fetch Dinah from the house of Shechem, and they went and came to the house of Shechem to take away Dinah from there.

(Jasher 33:13)

And when they came Shechem went out to them with his men and drove them from his house, and he would not suffer them to come before Dinah, but Shechem was sitting with Dinah kissing and embracing her before their eyes.

(Jasher 33:14)

And the servants of Jacob came back and told him, saying, When we came, he and his men drove us away, and thus Shechem did to Dinah before our eyes.

(...Genesis 34:5) (Jasher 33:15)

And Jacob knew moreover that Shechem had defiled his daughter, but he said nothing. Now his sons were with his cattle in the field: and Jacob held his peace until they were come.

(...Jasher 33:16)

And before his sons came home Jacob sent two maidens from his servants' daughters to take care of Dinah in the house of Shechem, and to remain with her.

(Genesis 34:6) (Jasher 33:19...)

And Hamor the father of Shechem went out to Jacob to commune with him concerning this matter.

(Genesis 34:7) (...Jasher 33:19, 20) (...Jubilees 30:3...)

And when he had gone from the house of his son Shechem, before he came to Jacob to speak to him, behold the sons of Jacob came out of the field when they heard the thing that Shechem the son of Hamor had done: and the men were very much grieved concerning their sister, and they were very wroth because of the men of Shechem; and they all came home fired with anger, before the time of gathering in their cattle, because he had wrought folly in Israel in lying with Jacob's daughter; which thing ought not to be done.

(Jasher 33:21)

And they came and sat before their father and they spoke to him kindled with wrath, saying, Surely death is due to this man and to his household, because the Lord God of the whole earth commanded Noah and his children that man shall never rob, nor commit adultery; now behold Shechem has both ravaged and committed fornication with our sister, and not one of all the people of the city spoke a word to him.

(Jasher 33:22)

Surely you know and understand that the judgment of death is due to Shechem, and to his father, and to the whole city on account of the thing which he has done.

(Jasher 33:23)

And while they were speaking before their father in this matter, behold Hamor the father of Shechem came to speak to Jacob the words of his son concerning Dinah, and he sat before Jacob and before his sons.

(Genesis 34:8) (Jasher 33:24...)

And Hamor communed with them, saying, The soul of my son Shechem longs for your daughter: I pray give her him to wife.

(Genesis 34:9) (...Jasher 33:24...)
And make marriages with us, and give your daughters to us, and take our daughters to you.

(Genesis 34:10) (...Jasher 33:24, 25)
And you shall dwell with us in our land: For our land is very extensive and the land shall be before you; dwell and trade therein, and get possessions therein and do therein as you desire, and no one shall prevent you by saying a word to you. And we will be as one people in the land.

(Jasher 33:26)
And Hamor ceased speaking to Jacob and his sons, and behold Shechem his son had come after him, and he sat before them.

(Genesis 34:11) (Jasher 33:27)
And Shechem said to her father and to her brothers, Let me find grace in your eyes that you will give me your daughter, and what you shall say to me I will give, that will I do for her.

(Genesis 34:12) (Jasher 33:28) (...Jubilees 30:3...)
Ask me never so much dowry and gift, and I will give according as you shall say to me: and whatever you shall say to me that will I do, and whoever he be that will rebel against your orders, he shall die; but give me the damsel to wife.

(Genesis 34:13) (Jasher 33:29...) (...Jubilees 30:3)
And the sons of Jacob, Simeon and Levi, answered Shechem and Hamor his father with evil intent and dealt deceitfully with them and beguiled them, and said, because he had defiled Dinah their sister: All you have spoken to us we will do for you.

(Jasher 33:30)
And behold our sister is in your house, but keep away from her until we send to our father Isaac concerning this matter, for we can do nothing without his consent.

(Jasher 33:31)
For he know the ways of our father Abraham, and whatever he says to us we will tell you, we will conceal nothing from you.

(Jasher 33:32)
And Simeon and Levi spoke this to Shechem and his father in order to find a pretext, and to seek counsel what was to be done to Shechem and to his city in this matter.

(Jasher 33:33)
And when Shechem and his father heard the words of Simeon and Levi, it seemed good in their sight, and Shechem and his father came forth to go home.

(Jasher 33:34)
And when they had gone, the sons of Jacob said to their father, saying, Behold, we know that death is due to these wicked ones and to their city, because they transgressed that which God had commanded to Noah and his children and his seed after them.

(Jasher 33:35)
And also because Shechem did this thing to our sister Dinah in defiling her, for such vileness shall never be done among us.

(Jasher 33:36)
Now therefore know and see what you will do, and seek

counsel and pretext what is to be done to them, in order to kill all the inhabitants of this city.

(Jasher 33:37)
And Simeon said to them, Here is a proper advice for you: tell them to circumcise every male among them as we are circumcised, and if they do not wish to do this, we shall take our daughter from them and go away.

(Jasher 33:38)
And if they consent to do this and will do it, then when they are sunk down with pain, we will attack them with our swords, as upon one who is quiet and peaceable, and we will slay every male person among them.

(Jasher 33:39)
And Simeon's advice pleased them, and Simeon and Levi resolved to do to them as it was proposed.

(Jasher 33:40)
And on the next morning Shechem and Hamor his father came again to Jacob and his sons, to speak concerning Dinah, and to hear what answer the sons of Jacob would give to their words.

(Jasher 33:41)
And the sons of Jacob spoke deceitfully to them, saying, We told our father Isaac all your words, and your words pleased him.

(Jasher 33:42)
But he spoke to us, saying, Thus Abraham his father commanded him from God the Lord of the whole earth, that any man who is not of his descendants that should wish to

take one of his daughters, shall cause every male belonging to him to be circumcised, as we are circumcised, and then we may give him our daughter for a wife.

(Genesis 34:14) (Jasher 33:43)
And they said to them, Now we have made known to you all our ways that our father spoke to us, for we cannot do this thing of which you spoke to us, to give our sister to one that is uncircumcised; for that were a reproach to us:

(Genesis 34:15) (Jasher 33:44...)
But in this will we consent to you: If you will be as we are, that every male of you be circumcised;

(Genesis 34:16) (...Jasher 33:44)
Then will we give our daughters to you, and we will take your daughters to us, and we will dwell with you, and we will become one people as you have spoken.

(Genesis 34:17) (Jasher 33:45)
But if you will not hearken to us, to have every male circumcised as we are circumcised, as we have commanded; then we will come to you, and take our daughter from you and we will be gone.

(Genesis 34:18) (Jasher 33:46...)
And Shechem and his father Hamor heard the words of the sons of Jacob, and their words pleased Hamor, and Shechem, Hamor's son, exceedingly.

(Genesis 34:19) (...Jasher 33:46)
And Shechem and his father Hamor hastened to do the wishes of the sons of Jacob. And the young man deferred not to do the thing, because he had delight in Jacob's daughter and his

soul was riveted to her: and he was more honorable than all the house of his father.

(Genesis 34:20) (Jasher 33:47)
And Hamor and Shechem his son hastened and came to the gate of their city, and they assembled all the men of their city and communed with the men of their city, and spoke to them the words of the sons of Jacob, saying,

(Genesis 34:21) (Jasher 33:48)
We came to these men, the sons of Jacob. These men are peaceable with us and we spoke to them concerning their daughter, and these men will consent to do according to our wishes; therefore, let them dwell in the land, and trade therein; for the land, behold, it is large enough for them; let us take their daughters to us for wives, and let us give them our daughters and we shall be one people.

(Genesis 34:22) (Jasher 33:49)
Only herein will the men consent to us to dwell with us, together with their cattle and possessions, to be one people, if every male among us be circumcised, as they are circumcised as their God commanded them, and when we shall have done according to their instructions to be circumcised.

(Genesis 34:23)
Shall not their cattle and their substance and every beast of theirs be ours? Only let us consent to them, and they will dwell with us.

(Genesis 34:24...) (Jasher 33:50...)
And when all the men of the city heard the words of Shechem and his father Hamor, then they were agreeable to this proposal; all that went out of the gate of his city hearkened

to Hamor and to Shechem his son for Shechem and his father Hamor were greatly esteemed by them, being the princes of the land.

(...Genesis 34:24) (...Jasher 33:50, 51)
And on the next day, Shechem and Hamor his father rose up early in the morning, and they assembled all the men of their city into the middle of the city, and they called for the sons of Jacob, who circumcised every male belonging to them on that day and the next. And every male was circumcised, all that went out of the gate of his city.

(Jasher 33:52)
And they circumcised Shechem and Hamor his father, and the five brothers of Shechem, and then everyone rose up and went home, for this thing was from the Lord against the city of Shechem, and Simeon's counsel in this matter was from the Lord, in order that the Lord might deliver the city of Shechem into the hands of Jacob's two sons.

~ ~ ~

(Jasher 34:1)
And the number of all the males that were circumcised, were six hundred and forty-five men, and two hundred and forty-six children.

(Jasher 34:2)
But Chiddekem, son of Pered, the father of Hamor, and his six brothers, would not listen to Shechem and his father Hamor, and they would not be circumcised, for the proposal of the

sons of Jacob was loathsome in their sight, and their anger was greatly roused at this, that the people of the city had not hearkened to them.

(Jasher 34:3)
And in the evening of the second day, they found eight small children who had not been circumcised, for their mothers had concealed them from Shechem and his father Hamor, and from the men of the city.

(Jasher 34:4)
And Shechem and his father Hamor sent to have them brought before them to be circumcised, when Chiddekem and his six brothers sprang at them with their swords, and sought to slay them.

(Jasher 34:5)
And they sought to slay also Shechem and his father Hamor and they sought to slay Dinah with them on account of this matter.

(Jasher 34:6)
And they said to them, What is this thing that you have done? Are there no women among the daughters of your brothers the Canaanites, that you wish to take to yourselves daughters of the Hebrews, whom ye knew not before, and will do this act which your fathers never commanded you?

(Jasher 34:7)
Do you imagine that you will succeed through this act which you have done? And what will you answer in this affair to your brothers the Canaanites, who will come tomorrow and ask you concerning this thing?

(Jasher 34:8)
And if your act shall not appear just and good in their sight, what will you do for your lives, and me for our lives, in your not having hearkened to our voices?

(Jasher 34:9)
And if the inhabitants of the land and all your brothers the children of Ham, shall hear of your act, saying,

(Jasher 34:10)
On account of a Hebrew woman Shechem and Hamor his father, and all the inhabitants of their city, did that with which they had been unacquainted and which their ancestors never commanded them, where then will you fly or where conceal your shame, all your days before your brothers, the inhabitants of the land of Canaan?

(Jasher 34:11)
Now therefore we cannot bear up against this thing which you have done, neither can we be burdened with this yoke upon us, which our ancestors did not command us.

(Jasher 34:12)
Behold tomorrow we will go and assemble all our brothers, the Canaanite brothers who dwell in the land, and we will all come and smite you and all those who trust in you, that there shall not be a remnant left from you or them.

(Jasher 34:13)
And when Hamor and his son Shechem and all the people of the city heard the words of Chiddekem and his brothers, they were terribly afraid of their lives at their words, and they repented of what they had done.

(Jasher 34:14)
And Shechem and his father Hamor answered their father Chiddekem and his brothers, and they said to them, All the words which you spoke to us are true.

(Jasher 34:15)
Now do not say, nor imagine in your hearts that on account of the love of the Hebrews we did this thing that our ancestors did not command us.

(Jasher 34:16)
But because we saw that it was not their intention and desire to accede to our wishes concerning their daughter as to our taking her, except on this condition, so we hearkened to their voices and did this act which you saw, in order to obtain our desire from them.

(Jasher 34:17)
And when we shall have obtained our request from them, we will then return to them and do to them that which you say to us.

(Jasher 34:18)
We beseech you then to wait and tarry until our flesh shall be healed and we again become strong, and we will then go together against them, and do to them that which is in your hearts and in ours.

(Jasher 34:19)
And Dinah the daughter of Jacob heard all these words which Chiddekem and his brothers had spoken, and what Hamor and his son Shechem and the people of their city had answered them.

(Jasher 34:20)
And she hastened and sent one of her maidens, that her father had sent to take care of her in the house of Shechem, to Jacob her father and to her brothers, saying:

(Jasher 34:21)
Thus Chiddekem and his brothers advised concerning you, and thus Hamor and Shechem and the people of the city answered them.

(Jasher 34:22)
And when Jacob heard these words he was filled with wrath, and he was indignant at them, and his anger was kindled against them.

(Jasher 34:23)
And Simeon and Levi swore and said, As the Lord lives, the God of the whole earth, by this time tomorrow, there shall not be a remnant left in the whole city.

(Genesis 34:25...) (Jubilees 30:4...)
And it came to pass on the third day, when they were sore, that two of the sons of Jacob, Simeon and Levi, Dinah's brothers, took each man his sword, and came unexpectedly on the city of Shechem boldly.

(Jasher 34:24)
And twenty young men had concealed themselves who were not circumcised, and these young men fought against Simeon and Levi, and Simeon and Levi killed eighteen of them, and two fled from them and escaped to some lime pits that were in the city, and Simeon and Levi sought for them, but could not find them.

(Jasher 34:25)
And Simeon and Levi continued to go about in the city, and they killed all the people of the city at the edge of the sword, and they left none remaining.

(Jasher 34:26)
And there was a great consternation in the midst of the city, and the cry of the people of the city ascended to heaven, and all the women and children cried aloud.

(...Genesis 34:25) (Jasher 34:27) (...Jubilees 30:4)
And Simeon and Levi executed judgment on all the men of Shechem, and slew all the men whom they found in the city; they did not leave a male remaining in the whole city. They slew all in torments because they had dishonored their sister Dinah.

(Jubilees 30:5)
And thus, let it not be done again from here after, that a daughter of Israel be defiled; for judgment is ordained in heaven against them that they should destroy with the sword all the men of the Shechemites because they had wrought shame in Israel.

(Jubilees 30:6)
And the Lord delivered them into the hands of the sons of Jacob that they might exterminate them with the sword and execute judgment on them, and that it might not thus again be done in Israel that a virgin of Israel should be defiled.

(Jubilees 30:7)
And if there is any man who wishes in Israel to give his daughter or his sister to any man who is of the seed of the Gentiles he shall surely die, and they shall stone him with stones; for he

has wrought shame in Israel; and they shall burn the woman with fire, because she has dishonored the name of the house of her father, and she shall be rooted out of Israel.

(Jubilees 30:8)
And let not an adulteress and no uncleanness be found in Israel throughout all the days of the generations of the earth; for Israel is holy to the Lord, and every man who has defiled it shall surely die: they shall stone him with stones.

(Jubilees 30:9)
For thus has it been ordained and written in the heavenly tablets regarding all the seed of Israel: he who defiles it shall surely die, and he shall be stoned with stones.

(Jubilees 30:10)
And to this law there is no limit of days, and no remission, nor any atonement: but the man who has defiled his daughter shall be rooted out in the midst of all Israel, because he has given of his seed to Moloch, and wrought impiously so as to defile it.

(Jubilees 30:11)
And do you, Moses, command the children of Israel and exhort them not to give their daughters to the Gentiles, and not to take for their sons any of the daughters of the Gentiles, for this is abominable before the Lord.

(Jubilees 30:12)
For this reason, I have written for you in the words of the Law all the deeds of the Shechemites, which they wrought against Dinah, and how the sons of Jacob spoke, saying: We will not give our daughter to a man who is uncircumcised; for that were a reproach to us.

(Jubilees 30:13)
And it is a reproach to Israel, to those who live, and to those that take the daughters of the Gentiles; for this is unclean and abominable to Israel.

(Jubilees 30:14)
And Israel will not be free from this uncleanness if it has a wife of the daughters of the Gentiles, or has given any of its daughters to a man who is of any of the Gentiles.

(Jubilees 30:15)
For there will be plague on plague, and curse on curse, and every judgment and plague and curse will come on him: if he does this thing, or hide his eyes from those who commit uncleanness, or those who defile the sanctuary of the Lord, or those who profane His holy name, then will the whole nation together be judged for all the uncleanness and profanation of this man.

(Jubilees 30:16)
And there will be no respect of persons and no receiving at his hands of fruits and offerings and burnt-offerings and fat, nor the fragrance of sweet savor, so as to accept it: and so every man or woman in Israel shall fare who defiles the sanctuary.

(Jubilees 30:17)
For this reason, I have commanded you, saying: Testify this testimony to Israel: see how the Shechemites fared and their sons: how they were delivered into the hands of two sons of Jacob, and they slew them under tortures, and it was reckoned to them for righteousness, and it is written down to them for righteousness.

(Jubilees 30:18)
And the seed of Levi was chosen for the priesthood, and to be Levites, that they might minister before the Lord, as we, continually, and that Levi and his sons may be blessed forever; for he was zealous to execute righteousness and judgment and vengeance on all those who arose against Israel.

(Jubilees 30:19)
And so, they inscribe as a testimony in his favor on the heavenly tablets blessing and righteousness before the God of all:

(Jubilees 30:20)
And we remember the righteousness which the man fulfilled during his life, at all periods of the year; until a thousand generations they will record it, and it will come to him and to his descendants after him, and he has been recorded on the heavenly tablets as a friend and a righteous man.

(Jubilees 30:21)
All this account I have written for you, and have commanded you to say to the children of Israel, that they should not commit sin nor transgress the ordinances nor break the covenant which has been ordained for them, that they should fulfill it and be recorded as friends.

(Jubilees 30:22)
But if they transgress and work uncleanness in every way, they will be recorded on the heavenly tablets as adversaries, and they will be destroyed out of the book of life, and they will be recorded in the book of those who will be destroyed and with those who will be rooted out of the earth.

(Jubilees 30:23)
And on the day when the sons of Jacob slew Shechem a writing was recorded in their favor in heaven that they had executed righteousness and uprightness and vengeance on the sinners, and it was written for a blessing.

(Genesis 34:26) (Jasher 34:28) (Jubilees 30:24...)
And they slew Hamor and Shechem his son with the edge of the sword, and took Dinah, their sister, out of Shechem's house, and went out from there.

(Genesis 34:27) (Jasher 34:29...)
And the sons of Jacob went and returned, and came on the slain, and spoiled all their property which was in the city, because they had defiled their sister.

(Jasher 34:30)
And while they were taking the spoil, three hundred men stood up and threw dust at them and struck them with stones, when Simeon turned to them and he slew them all with the edge of the sword, and Simeon turned before Levi, and came into the city.

(Genesis 34:28) (...Jasher 34:29, 31...) (...Jubilees 30:24...)
And they took away captive everything that was in Shechem, their sheep, and their oxen, and their cattle, and their donkeys, and that which was in the city, and that which was in the field.

(Genesis 34:29) (...Jasher 34:31) (...Jubilees 30:24)
And all their wealth, and all their flocks, and all their little ones, and also the remainder of their wives took they captive, and spoiled even all that was in the house; and they led all these away, and they opened a gate and went out and came and brought them all to their father Jacob with vigor.

(Jasher 34:32)
And when Jacob saw all that they had done to the city, and saw the spoil that they took from them, Jacob was very angry at them, and Jacob said to them, What is this that you have done to me? Behold I obtained rest among the Canaanite inhabitants of the land, and none of them meddled with me.

(Jubilees 30:25)
And he reproached them because they had put the city to the sword for he feared those who dwelt in the land, the Canaanites and the Perizzites.

(Genesis 34:30) (Jasher 34:33)
And Jacob said to Simeon and Levi, You have troubled me to make me to stink among the inhabitants of the land, among the Canaanites and the Perizzites: and I being few in number, they shall gather themselves together against me, and slay me when they hear of your work with their brothers; and I shall be destroyed, I and my house.

(Genesis 34:31) (Jasher 34:34)
And Simeon and Levi and all their brothers with them answered their father Jacob and said to him, Behold we live in the land, and shall Shechem do this to our sister? Why are you silent at all that Shechem has done? Should he deal with our sister as with a harlot in the streets?

(Jasher 34:35)
And the number of women whom Simeon and Levi took captives from the city of Shechem, whom they did not slay, was eighty-five who had not known man.

(Jasher 34:36)
And among them was a young damsel of beautiful appearance

and well favored, whose name was Bunah, and Simeon took her for a wife, and the number of the males which they took captives and did not slay, was forty-seven men, and the rest they slew.

(Jasher 34:37)
And all the young men and women that Simeon and Levi had taken captives from the city of Shechem, were servants to the sons of Jacob and to their children after them, until the day of the sons of Jacob going forth from the land of Egypt.

(Jasher 34:38)
And when Simeon and Levi had gone forth from the city, the two young men that were left, who had concealed themselves in the city, and did not die among the people of the city, rose up, and these young men went into the city and walked about in it, and found the city desolate without man, and only women weeping, and these young men cried out and said, Behold, this is the evil which the sons of Jacob the Hebrew did to this city in their having this day destroyed one of the Canaanite cities, and were not afraid of their lives of all the land of Canaan.

(Jasher 34:39)
And these men left the city and went to the city of Tapnach, and they came there and told the inhabitants of Tapnach all that had befallen them, and all that the sons of Jacob had done to the city of Shechem.

(Jasher 34:40)
And the information reached Jashub king of Tapnach, and he sent men to the city of Shechem to see those young men, for the king did not believe them in this account, saying, How could two men lay waste such a large town as Shechem?

(Jasher 34:41)
And the messengers of Jashub came back and told him, saying, We came to the city, and it is destroyed, there is not a man there; only weeping women; neither is any flock or cattle there, for all that was in the city the sons of Jacob took away.

(Jasher 34:42)
And Jashub wondered at this, saying, How could two men do this thing, to destroy so large a city, and not one man able to stand against them?

(Jasher 34:43)
For the like has not been from the days of Nimrod, and not even from the remotest time, has the like taken place; and Jashub, king of Tapnach, said to his people, Be courageous and we will go and fight against these Hebrews, and do to them as they did to the city, and we will avenge the cause of the people of the city.

(Jasher 34:44)
And Jashub, king of Tapnach, consulted with his counselors about this matter, and his advisers said to him, Alone you will not prevail over the Hebrews, for they must be powerful to do this work to the whole city.

(Jasher 34:45)
If two of them laid waste the whole city, and no one stood against them, surely if you will go against them, they will all rise against us and destroy us likewise.

(Jasher 34:46)
But if you will send to all the kings that surround us, and let them come together, then we will go with them and fight against the sons of Jacob; then will you prevail against them.

(Jasher 34:47)
And Jashub heard the words of his counselors, and their words pleased him and his people, and he did so; and Jashub king of Tapnach sent to all the kings of the Amorites that surrounded Shechem and Tapnach, saying,

(Jasher 34:48)
Go up with me and assist me, and we will smite Jacob the Hebrew and all his sons, and destroy them from the earth, for thus he did to the city of Shechem, and do you not know of it?

(Jasher 34:49)
And all the kings of the Amorites heard the evil that the sons of Jacob had done to the city of Shechem, and they were greatly astonished at them.

(Jasher 34:50)
And the seven kings of the Amorites assembled with all their armies, about ten thousand men with drawn swords, and they came to fight against the sons of Jacob; and Jacob heard that the kings of the Amorites had assembled to fight against his sons, and Jacob was greatly afraid, and it distressed him.

(Jasher 34:51)
And Jacob exclaimed against Simeon and Levi, saying, What is this act that you did? Why have you injured me, to bring against me all the children of Canaan to destroy me and my household? For I was at rest, even I and my household, and you have done this thing to me, and provoked the inhabitants of the land against me by your proceedings.

(Jasher 34:52)
And Judah answered his father, saying, Was it for naught my brothers Simeon and Levi killed all the inhabitants of

Shechem? Surely it was because Shechem had humbled our sister, and transgressed the command of our God to Noah and his children, for Shechem took our sister away by force, and committed adultery with her.

(Jasher 34:53)
And Shechem did all this evil and not one of the inhabitants of his city interfered with him, to say, Why will you do this? Surely for this my brothers went and smote the city, and the Lord delivered it into their hands, because its inhabitants had transgressed the commands of our God. Is it then for naught that they have done all this?

(Jasher 34:54)
And now why are you afraid or distressed, and why are you displeased at my brothers, and why is your anger kindled against them?

(Jasher 34:55)
Surely our God who delivered into their hand the city of Shechem and its people, he will also deliver into our hands all the Canaanite kings who are coming against us, and we will do to them as my brothers did to Shechem.

(Jasher 34:56)
Now be tranquil about them and cast away your fears, but trust in the Lord our God, and pray to him to assist us and deliver us, and deliver our enemies into our hands.

(Jasher 34:57)
And Judah called to one of his father's servants, Go now and see where those kings, who are coming against us, are situated with their armies.

(Jasher 34:58)
And the servant went and looked far off, and went up opposite Mount Sihon, and saw all the camps of the kings standing in the fields, and he returned to Judah and said, Behold the kings are situated in the field with all their camps, a people exceedingly numerous, like to the sand upon the sea shore.

(Jasher 34:59)
And Judah said to Simeon and Levi, and to all his brothers, Strengthen yourselves and be sons of valor, for the Lord our God is with us, do not fear them.

(Jasher 34:60)
Stand forth each man, girt with his weapons of war, his bow and his sword, and we will go and fight against these uncircumcised men; the Lord is our God, He will save us.

(Jasher 34:61)
And they rose up, and each girt on his weapons of war, great and small, eleven sons of Jacob, and all the servants of Jacob with them.

(Jasher 34:62)
And all the servants of Isaac who were with Isaac in Hebron, all came to them equipped in all sorts of war instruments, and the sons of Jacob and their servants, being one hundred and twelve men, went towards these kings, and Jacob also went with them.

(Jasher 34:63)
And the sons of Jacob sent to their father Isaac the son of Abraham to Hebron, the same is Kireath-arba, saying,

(Jasher 34:64)
Pray we beseech you for us to the Lord our God, to protect us from the hands of the Canaanites who are coming against us, and to deliver them into our hands.

(Jasher 34:65)
And Isaac the son of Abraham prayed to the Lord for his sons, and he said, O Lord God, you promised my father, saying, I will multiply your seed as the stars of heaven, and you also promised me, and establish you your word, now that the kings of Canaan are coming together, to make war with my children because they committed no violence.

(Jasher 34:66)
Now therefore, O Lord God, God of the whole earth, pervert, I pray you, the counsel of these kings that they may not fight against my sons.

(Jasher 34:67)
And impress the hearts of these kings and their people with the terror of my sons and bring down their pride, and that they may turn away from my sons.

(Jasher 34:68)
And with your strong hand and outstretched arm deliver my sons and their servants from them, for power and might are in your hands to do all this.

(Jasher 34:69)
And the sons of Jacob and their servants went toward these kings, and they trusted in the Lord their God, and while they were going, Jacob their father also prayed to the Lord and said, O Lord God, powerful and exalted God, who has reigned from days of old, from thence till now and forever;

(Jasher 34:70)
You are He who stirs up wars and causes them to cease, in your hand are power and might to exalt and to bring down; O may my prayer be acceptable before you that you mayest turn to me with your mercies, to impress the hearts of these kings and their people with the terror of my sons, and terrify them and their camps, and with your great kindness deliver all those that trust in you, for it is you who can bring people under us and reduce nations under our power.

~ ~ ~

(Jasher 35:1)
And all the kings of the Amorites came and took their stand in the field to consult with their counselors what was to be done with the sons of Jacob, for they were still afraid of them, saying, Behold, two of them slew the whole of the city of Shechem.

(Jasher 35:2)
And the Lord heard the prayers of Isaac and Jacob, and he filled the hearts of all these kings' advisers with great fear and terror that they unanimously exclaimed,

(Jasher 35:3)
Are you silly this day, or is there no understanding in you, that you will fight with the Hebrews, and why will you take a delight in your own destruction this day?

(Jasher 35:4)
Behold two of them came to the city of Shechem without fear or terror, and they killed all the inhabitants of the city, that no

man stood up against them, and how will you be able to fight with them all?

(Jasher 35:5)
Surely you know that their God is exceedingly fond of them, and has done mighty things for them, such as have not been done from days of old, and among all the gods of nations, there is none can do like to his mighty deeds.

(Jasher 35:6)
Surely, he delivered their father Abraham, the Hebrew, from the hand of Nimrod, and from the hand of all his people who had many times sought to slay him.

(Jasher 35:7)
He delivered him also from the fire in which king Nimrod had cast him, and his God delivered him from it.

(Jasher 35:8)
And who else can do the like? Surely it was Abraham who slew the five kings of Elam, when they had touched his brother's son who in those days dwelt in Sodom.

(Jasher 35:9)
And took his servant that was faithful in his house and a few of his men, and they pursued the kings of Elam in one night and killed them, and restored to his brother's son all his property which they had taken from him.

(Jasher 35:10)
And surely you know the God of these Hebrews is much delighted with them, and they are also delighted with him, for they know that he delivered them from all their enemies.

(Jasher 35:11)
And behold through his love toward his God, Abraham took his only and precious son and intended to bring him up as a burnt offering to his God, and had it not been for God who prevented him from doing this, he would then have done it through his love to his God.

(Jasher 35:12)
And God saw all his works, and swore to him, and promised him that he would deliver his sons and all his seed from every trouble that would befall them, because he had done this thing, and through his love to his God stifled his compassion for his child.

(Jasher 35:13)
And have you not heard what their God did to Pharaoh king of Egypt, and to Abimelech king of Gerar, through taking Abraham's wife, who said of her, She is my sister, lest they might slay him on account of her, and think of taking her for a wife? And God did to them and their people all that you heard of.

(Jasher 35:14)
And behold, we ourselves saw with our eyes that Esau, the brother of Jacob, came to him with four hundred men, with the intention of slaying him, for he called to mind that he had taken away from him his father's blessing.

(Jasher 35:15)
And he went to meet him when he came from Syria, to smite the mother with the children, and who delivered him from his hands but his God in whom he trusted? He delivered him from the hand of his brother and also from the hands of his enemies, and surely, he again will protect them.

(Jasher 35:16)
Who does not know that it was their God who inspired them with strength to do to the town of Shechem the evil which you heard of?

(Jasher 35:17)
Could it then be with their own strength that two men could destroy such a large city as Shechem had it not been for their God in whom they trusted? He said and did to them all this to slay the inhabitants of the city in their city.

(Jasher 35:18)
And can you then prevail over them who have come forth together from your city to fight with the whole of them, even if a thousand times as many more should come to your assistance?

(Jasher 35:19)
Surely you know and understand that you do not come to fight with them, but you come to war with their God who made choice of them, and you have therefore all come this day to be destroyed.

(Jasher 35:20)
Now therefore refrain from this evil which you are endeavoring to bring upon yourselves, and it will be better for you not to go to battle with them, although they are but few in numbers, because their God is with them.

(Jasher 35:21) (Jubilees 30:26)
And when the kings of the Amorites heard all the words of their advisers, their hearts were filled with terror. And the dread of the Lord was on all the cities which are around about Shechem, and they were afraid of the sons of Jacob and would

not fight against them. And they did not rise to pursue after the sons of Jacob; for terror had fallen on them.

(Jasher 35:22)
And they inclined their ears to the words of their advisers, and they listened to all their words, and the words of the counselors greatly pleased the kings, and they did so.

(Jasher 35:23)
And the kings turned and refrained from the sons of Jacob, for they durst not approach them to make war with them, for they were greatly afraid of them, and their hearts melted within them from their fear of them.

(Jasher 35:24)
For this proceeded from the Lord to them, for he heard the prayers of his servants Isaac and Jacob, for they trusted in him; and all these kings returned with their camps on that day, each to his own city, and they did not at that time fight with the sons of Jacob.

(Jasher 35:25)
And the sons of Jacob kept their station that day till evening opposite mount Sihon, and seeing that these kings did not come to fight against them, the sons of Jacob returned home.

Genesis: Chapter Thirty-Five

(Genesis 35:1) (Jasher 36:1)

And at that time the Lord God appeared and said to Jacob, Arise, go up to Bethel, and dwell there: and make there an altar to the Lord God, that appeared to you , who delivered you and your sons from affliction when you fled from the face of Esau your brother.

(Genesis 35:2) (Jubilees 31:1...)

And on the new moon of the month, Jacob said to his household, and to all that were with him, Put away the strange gods that are among you, and be clean, and change your garments:

(Genesis 35:3) (...Jubilees 31:1)

And let us arise, and go up to Bethel where I vowed a vow to Him on the day when I fled from the face of Esau my brother; and I will make there an altar to God, who answered me in the day of my distress, and was with me in the way which I went and brought me into this land in peace.

(Genesis 35:4) (Jubilees 31:2)

And they gave to Jacob all the strange gods which were in their hand, and all their earrings which were in their ears and which was on their necks and the idols which Rachel stole from Laban her father she gave wholly to Jacob. And he burnt and brake them to pieces and destroyed them; and Jacob hid them under the oak which was in the land of Shechem.

(Genesis 35:5)

And they journeyed: and the terror of God was on the cities

that were round about them, and they did not pursue after the sons of Jacob.

(Genesis 35:6) (Jasher 36:2)
So Jacob rose up with his sons and all belonging to him, and they went and came to Luz, which is in the land of Canaan, that is, Bethel, he and all the people that were with him, according to the word of the Lord.

(Genesis 35:7) (Jasher 36:3...) (Jubilees 31:3)
And Jacob was ninety-nine years old when he went up on the new moon of the seventh month to Bethel, and Jacob and his sons and all the people that were with him, remained in Bethel in Luz, and he built there an altar at the place where he had slept, to the Lord who appeared to him, and he set up a pillar there, and called the place El Bethel: because God appeared to him there, when he fled from the face of his brother. And he sent word to his father Isaac to come to him to his sacrifice, and to his mother Rebecca.

(Jubilees 31:4)
And Isaac said: Let my son Jacob come, and let me see him before I die.

(Jubilees 31:5)
And Jacob went to his father Isaac and to his mother Rebecca, to the house of his father Abraham, and he took two of his sons with him, Levi and Judah, and he came to his father Isaac and to his mother Rebecca.

(Jubilees 31:6)
And Rebecca came forth from the tower to the front of it to kiss Jacob and embrace him; for her spirit had revived when she heard: Behold Jacob your son has come; and she kissed him.

(Jubilees 31:7)
And she saw his two sons, and she recognized them, and said to him: Are these your sons, my son? And she embraced them and kissed them, and blessed them, saying: In you shall the seed of Abraham become illustrious, and you shall prove a blessing on the earth.

(Jubilees 31:8)
And Jacob went in to Isaac his father, to the chamber where he lay, and his two sons were with him, and he took the hand of his father, and stooping down he kissed him, and Isaac clung to the neck of Jacob his son, and wept on his neck.

(Jubilees 31:9)
And the darkness left the eyes of Isaac, and he saw the two sons of Jacob, Levi, and Judah, and he said: Are these your sons, my son? For they are like you.

(Jubilees 31:10)
And he said to him that they were truly his sons: And you have truly seen that they are truly my sons.

(Jubilees 31:11)
And they came near to him, and he turned and kissed them and embraced them both together.

(Jubilees 31:12)
And the spirit of prophecy came down into his mouth, and he took Levi by his right hand and Judah by his left.

(Jubilees 31:13)
And he turned to Levi first, and began to bless him first, and said to him: May the God of all, the very Lord of all the ages, bless you and your children throughout all the ages.

(Jubilees 31:14)
And may the Lord give to you and to your seed greatness and great glory, and cause you and your seed, from among all flesh, to approach Him to serve in His sanctuary as the angels of the presence and as the holy ones. (Even) as they, shall the seed of your sons be for glory and greatness and holiness, and may He make them great to all the ages.

(Jubilees 31:15)
And they shall be judges and princes, and chiefs of all the seed of the sons of Jacob; They shall speak the word of the Lord in righteousness. And they shall judge all His judgments in righteousness. And they shall declare My ways to Jacob and My paths to Israel. The blessing of the Lord shall be given in their mouths to bless all the seed of the beloved.

(Jubilees 31:16)
Your mother has called your name Levi, and justly has she called your name; You shall be joined to the Lord And be the companion of all the sons of Jacob; Let His table be yours, And do you and your sons eat thereof; And may your table be full to all generations, And your food not fail to all the ages.

(Jubilees 31:17)
And let all who hate you fall down before you, and let all your adversaries be rooted out and perish; And blessed be he that blesses you, and cursed be every nation that curses you.

(Jubilees 31:18)
And to Judah he said: May the Lord give you strength and power to tread down all that hate you; A prince shall you be, you and one of your sons, over the sons of Jacob; May your name and the name of your sons go forth and traverse every land and region. Then shall the Gentiles fear before your face, and all the nations shall quake.

(Jubilees 31:19)
In you shall be the help of Jacob, and in you be found the salvation of Israel.

(Jubilees 31:20)
And when you sit on the throne of honor of your righteousness there shall be great peace for all the seed of the sons of the beloved; Blessed be he that blesses you, and all that hate you and afflict you and curse yous shall be rooted out and destroyed from the earth and be accursed.

(Jubilees 31:21)
And turning he kissed him again and embraced him, and rejoiced greatly; for he had seen the sons of Jacob his son in very truth.

(Jubilees 31:22)
And he went forth from between his feet and fell down and bowed down to him, and he blessed them and rested there with Isaac his father that night, and they eat and drank with joy.

(Jubilees 31:23)
And he made the two sons of Jacob sleep, the one on his right hand and the other on his left, and it was counted to him for righteousness.

(Jubilees 31:24)
And Jacob told his father everything during the night, how the Lord had shown him great mercy, and how he had prospered all his ways, and protected him from all evil.

(Jubilees 31:25)
And Isaac blessed the God of his father Abraham, who had

not withdrawn his mercy and his righteousness from the sons of his servant Isaac.

(Jubilees 31:26)
And in the morning Jacob told his father Isaac the vow which he had vowed to the Lord, and the vision which he had seen, and that he had built an altar, and that everything was ready for the sacrifice to be made before the Lord as he had vowed, and that he had come to set him on a donkey.

(Jubilees 31:27)
And Isaac said to Jacob his son: I am not able to go with you; for I am old and not able to bear the way: go, my son, in peace; for I am one hundred and sixty-five years this day; I am no longer able to journey; set your mother on a donkey and let her go with you.

(Jubilees 31:28)
And I know, my son, that you have come on my account, and may this day be blessed on which you have seen me alive, and I also have seen you, my son.

(Jubilees 31:29)
May you prosper and fulfill the vow which you have vowed; and put not off your vow; for you shall be called to account as touching the vow; now therefore make haste to perform it, and may He be pleased who has made all things, to whom you have vowed the vow.

(Jubilees 31:30)
And he said to Rebecca: Go with Jacob your son; and Rebecca went with Jacob her son, and Deborah with her, and they came to Bethel.

(Jubilees 31:31)
And Jacob remembered the prayer with which his father had blessed him and his two sons, Levi and Judah, and he rejoiced and blessed the God of his fathers, Abraham and Isaac.

(Jubilees 31:32)
And he said: Now I know that I have an eternal hope, and my sons also, before the God of all; and thus it is ordained concerning the two; and they record it as an eternal testimony to them on the heavenly tablets how Isaac blessed them.

~ ~ ~

(Jubilees 32:1)
And he abode that night at Bethel, and Levi dreamed that they had ordained and made him the priest of the Most High God, him and his sons forever; and he awoke from his sleep and blessed the Lord.

(Jubilees 32:2)
And Jacob rose early in the morning, on the fourteenth of this month, and he gave a tithe of all that came with him, both of men and cattle, both of gold and every vessel and garment, yea, he gave tithes of all.

(...Jasher 31:3)
And Jacob and his sons remained in Bethel six months.

(...Jasher 36:8...) (Jubilees 32:3)
And in those days Rachel became pregnant with her son Benjamin. And Jacob counted his sons from him upwards

and Levi fell to the portion of the Lord, and his father clothed him in the garments of the priesthood and filled his hands.

(Jubilees 32:4)
And on the fifteenth of this month, he brought to the altar fourteen oxen from among the cattle, and twenty-eight rams, and forty-nine sheep, and seven lambs, and twenty-one kids of the goats as a burnt-offering on the altar of sacrifice, well pleasing for a sweet savor before God.

(Jubilees 32:5)
This was his offering, in consequence of the vow which he had vowed that he would give a tenth, with their fruit-offerings and their drink- offerings.

(Jubilees 32:6)
And when the fire had consumed it, he burnt incense on the fire over the fire, and for a thank-offering two oxen and four rams and four sheep, four he-goats, and two sheep of a year old, and two kids of the goats; and thus he did daily for seven days.

(Jubilees 32:7)
And he and all his sons and his men were eating with joy there during seven days and blessing and thanking the Lord, who had delivered him out of all his tribulation and had given him his vow.

(Jubilees 32:8)
And he tithed all the clean animals, and made a burnt sacrifice, but the unclean animals he gave not to Levi his son, and he gave him all the souls of the men.

(Jubilees 32:9)
And Levi discharged the priestly office at Bethel before Jacob his father in preference to his ten brothers, and he was a priest there, and Jacob gave his vow: thus, he tithed again the tithe to the Lord and sanctified it, and it became holy to Him.

(Jubilees 32:10)
And for this reason, it is ordained on the heavenly tablets as a law for the tithing again the tithe to eat before the Lord from year to year, in the place where it is chosen that His name should dwell, and to this law there is no limit of days forever.

(Jubilees 32:11)
This ordinance is written that it may be fulfilled from year to year in eating the second tithe before the Lord in the place where it has been chosen, and nothing shall remain over from it from this year to the year following.

(Jubilees 32:12)
For in its year shall the seed be eaten till the days of the gathering of the seed of the year, and the wine till the days of the wine, and the oil till the days of its season.

(Jubilees 32:13)
And all that is left thereof and becomes old, let it be regarded as polluted: let it be burnt with fire, for it is unclean.

(Jubilees 32:14)
And thus, let them eat it together in the sanctuary, and let them not suffer it to become old.

(Jubilees 32:15)
And all the tithes of the oxen and sheep shall be holy to the Lord, and shall belong to his priests, which they will eat before

Him from year to year; for thus is it ordained and engraved regarding the tithe on the heavenly tablets.

(Jubilees 32:16)
And on the following night, on the twenty-second day of this month, Jacob resolved to build that place, and to surround the court with a wall, and to sanctify it and make it holy forever, for himself and his children after him.

(Genesis 35:9) (Jasher 36:8...) (Jubilees 32:17...)
And Jacob was a hundred years old when the Lord God appeared to Jacob again by night, when he came out of Padanaram, and blessed him.

(Genesis 35:10) (...Jasher 36:8) (...Jubilees 32:17)
And God said to him, Your name is Jacob: your name shall not be called Jacob anymore, but your name shall be Israel: and he called his name Israel.

(Genesis 35:11) (Jubilees 32:18)
And God said to him again: I am the Lord God Almighty who created the heaven and the earth: and I will increase you and multiply you exceedingly; a nation and a company of nations shall be of you, and kings shall come out of your loins; and they shall judge everywhere wherever the foot of the sons of men has trodden.

(Genesis 35:12)
And the land which I gave Abraham and Isaac, to you I will give it, and to your seed after you will I give the land.

(Jubilees 32:19)
And I will give to your seed all the earth which is under heaven,

and they shall judge all the nations according to their desires, and after that they shall get possession of the whole earth and inherit it forever.

(Genesis 35:13) (Jubilees 32:20)
And He finished speaking with him, and God went up from him in the place where he talked with him. And Jacob looked till He had ascended into heaven.

(Jubilees 32:21)
And he saw in a vision of the night, and behold an angel descended from heaven with seven tablets in his hands, and he gave them to Jacob, and he read them and knew all that was written therein which would befall him and his sons throughout all the ages.

(Jubilees 32:22)
And he showed him all that was written on the tablets, and said to him: Do not build this place, and do not make it an eternal sanctuary, and do not dwell here; for this is not the place. Go to the house of Abraham your father and dwell with Isaac your father until the day of the death of your father.

(Jubilees 32:23)
For in Egypt you shall die in peace, and you shall be buried in this land with honor in the sepulcher of your fathers, with Abraham and Isaac.

(Jubilees 32:24)
Fear not, for as you have seen and read it, thus shall it all be; and do you write do

(Jubilees 32:25)
And Jacob said: Lord, how can I remember all that I have

read and seen? And he said to him: I will bring all things to your remembrance.

(Jubilees 32:26)
And he went up from him, and he awoke from his sleep, and he remembered everything which he had read and seen, and he wrote down all the words which he had read and seen.

(Jubilees 32:27)
And he celebrated there yet another day, and he sacrificed thereon according to all that he sacrificed on the former days, and called its name 'Addition,' for this day was added and the former days he called 'The Feast'.

(Jubilees 32:28)
And thus, it was manifested that it should be, and it is written on the heavenly tablets: wherefore it was revealed to him that he should celebrate it, and add it to the seven days of the feast.

(Jubilees 32:29)
And its name was called 'Addition,' because that it was recorded among the days of the feast days, according to the number of the days of the year.

(Genesis 35:14)
And Jacob set up a pillar in the place where he talked with him, even a pillar of stone: and he poured a drink offering thereon, and he poured oil thereon.

(Genesis 35:15)
And Jacob called the name of the place where God spoke with him, Bethel.

(*Genesis 35:8) (Jasher 36:4, 6...) (Jubilees 32:30)
But at that time, in the night, on the twenty-third of this month, Deborah, the daughter of Uz, Rebekah's nurse who had been with Jacob, died. And she was buried beneath the city of Bethel under an oak of the river: and he called the name of this place: 'The river of Deborah,' and the name of the oak was called Allonbachuth, 'The oak of the mourning of Deborah.'

* This verse was displaced for a better understanding of the chronology of events throughout this passage.

(Jubilees 32:31)
And Rebecca went and returned to her house to his father Isaac, and Jacob sent by her hand rams and sheep and he-goats that she should prepare a meal for his father such as he desired.

(Genesis 35:16...) (Jasher 36:9, 10...) (Jubilees 32:32...)
And at that time Jacob and all belonging to him journeyed from Bethel, and he went after his mother to go to his father's house, to Hebron.

(Jubilees 35:1)
And in the first year of the first week of the forty-fifth jubilee, Rebecca called Jacob, her son, and commanded him regarding his father and regarding his brother, that he should honor them all the days of his life.

(Jubilees 35:2)
And Jacob said: I will do everything as you have commanded me; for this thing will be honor and greatness to me, and righteousness before the Lord, that I should honor them.

(Jubilees 35:3)
And you too, mother, know from the time I was born until this day, all my deeds and all that is in my heart, that I always think good concerning all.

(Jubilees 35:4)
And how should I not do this thing which you have commanded me, that I should honor my father and my brother!

(Jubilees 35:5)
Tell me, mother, what perversity have you seen in me and I shall turn away from it, and mercy will be on me.

(Jubilees 35:6)
And she said to him: My son, I have not seen in you all my days any perverse but only upright deeds. And yet I will tell you the truth, my son: I shall die this year, and I shall not survive this year in my life; for I have seen in a dream the day of my death, that I should not live beyond a hundred and fifty-five years: and behold I have completed all the days of my life which I am to live.

(Jubilees 35:7)
And Jacob laughed at the words of his mother. Because his mother had said to him that she should die; and she was sitting opposite to him in possession of her strength, and she was not infirm in her strength; for she went in and out and saw, and her teeth were strong, and no ailment had touched her all the days of her life.

(Jubilees 35:8)
And Jacob said to her: Blessed am I, mother, if my days approach the days of your life, and my strength remain with me thus as your strength: and you will not die, for you are

jesting idly with me regarding your death.

(Jubilees 35:9)
And she went in to Isaac and said to him: One petition I make to you: make Esau swear that he will not injure Jacob, nor pursue him with enmity; for you know Esau's thoughts that they are perverse from his youth, and there is no goodness in him; for he desires after your death to kill him.

(Jubilees 35:10)
And you know all that he has done since the day Jacob his brother went to Haran until this day: how he has forsaken us with his whole heart, and has done evil to us; your flocks he has taken to himself, and carried off all your possessions from before your face.

(Jubilees 35:11)
And when we implored and besought him for what was our own, he did as a man who was taking pity on us.

(Jubilees 35:12)
And he is bitter against you because you blessed Jacob your perfect and upright son; for there is no evil but only goodness in him, and since he came from Haran to this day he has not robbed us of aught, for he brings us everything in its season always, and rejoices with all his heart when we take at his hands and he blesses us, and has not parted from us since he came from Haran until this day, and he remains with us continually at home honoring us.

(Jubilees 35:13)
And Isaac said to her: I, too, know and see the deeds of Jacob who is with us, how that with all his heart he honors us; but I loved Esau formerly more than Jacob, because he was the

firstborn; but now I love Jacob more than Esau, for he has done manifold evil deeds, and there is no righteousness in him, for all his ways are unrighteousness and violence.

(Jubilees 35:14)
And now my heart is troubled because of all his deeds, and neither he nor his seed is to be saved, for they are those who will be destroyed from the earth and who will be rooted out from under heaven, for he has forsaken the God of Abraham and gone after his wives and after their uncleanness and after their error, he and his children.

(Jubilees 35:15)
And you bid me to make him swear that he will not slay Jacob his brother; even if he swears, he will not abide by his oath, and he will not do good but evil only.

(Jubilees 35:16)
But if he desires to slay Jacob, his brother, into Jacob's hands will he be given, and he will not escape from his hands.

(Jubilees 35:17)
And fear you not on account of Jacob; for the guardian of Jacob is great and powerful and honored, and praised more than the guardian of Esau.

(Jubilees 35:18)
And Rebecca sent and called Esau and he came to her, and she said to him: I have a petition, my son, to make to you, and do you promise to do it, my son.

(Jubilees 35:19)
And he said: I will do everything that you say to me, and I will not refuse your petition.

(Jubilees 35:20)
And she said to him: I ask you that the day I die, you will take me in and bury me near Sarah, your father's mother, and that you and Jacob will love each other and that neither will desire evil against the other, but mutual love only, and you will prosper, my sons, and be honored in the midst of the land, and no enemy will rejoice over you, and you will be a blessing and a mercy in the eyes of all those that love you.

(Jubilees 35:21)
And he said: I will do all that you have told me, and I shall bury you on the day you die near Sarah, my father's mother, as you have desired that her bones may be near your bones.

(Jubilees 35:22)
And Jacob, my brother, also, I shall love above all flesh; for I have not a brother in all the earth but him only: and this is no great merit for me if I love him; for he is my brother, and we were sown together in your body, and together came we forth from your womb, and if I do not love my brother, whom shall I love?

(Jubilees 35:23)
And I, myself, beg you to exhort Jacob concerning me and concerning my sons, for I know that he will assuredly be king over me and my sons, for on the day my father blessed him he made him the higher and me the lower.

(Jubilees 35:24)
And I swear to you that I shall love him, and not desire evil against him all the days of my life but good only.

(Jubilees 35:25)
And he swore to her regarding all this matter. And she called

Jacob before the eyes of Esau, and gave him commandment according to the words which she had spoken to Esau.

(Jubilees 35:26)
And he said: I shall do your pleasure; believe me that no evil will proceed from me or from my sons against Esau, and I shall be first in naught save in love only.

(Jasher 36:5) (Jubilees 35:27)
And they ate and drank, she and her sons that night. And Rebecca the daughter of Bethuel, the mother of Jacob, died at that time, three jubilees and one week and one year old on that night, in Hebron, the same is Kireath-arba, and her two sons, Esau and Jacob, buried her in the double cave of Machpelah which Abraham had bought from the children of Heth, near Sarah, their father's mother.

(...Jasher 36:6)
And the life of Rebecca was one hundred and thirty-three years, and she died and when Jacob heard that his mother Rebecca was dead he wept bitterly for his mother, and made a great mourning for her, and for Deborah her nurse beneath the oak.

(Jasher 36:7)
And Laban the Syrian died in those days, for God smote him because he transgressed the covenant that existed between him and Jacob.

(...Genesis 35:16) (Jasher 36:9, 10...) (...Jubilees 32:32)
And while they were going on the road, he came to the land of Kabratan, and he dwelt there, and there was but a little way to come to Ephrath: and Rachel travailed, and she had hard labor.

(Genesis 35:17) (...Jasher 36:10...) (Jubilees 32:33...)
And it came to pass, when she was in hard labor, that the midwife said to her, Fear not; you shall have this son also. And Rachel bare a son in the night.

(Genesis 35:18) (Jasher 36:12) (...Jubilees 32:33)
And it came to pass, as her soul was in departing, (for she died) that she called his name Benoni, 'Son of my sorrow'; for she suffered in giving him birth: but Jacob his father called the name of his son that was born to him, which Rachel bare to him, Benjamin, for he was born to him in the land on the right hand on the eleventh of the eighth month in the first of the sixth week of this jubilee.

(Genesis 35:19) (...Jasher 36:10, 11...) (Jubilees 32:34...)
And Rachel died there, and was buried in the land in the way to Ephrath, which is Bethlehem.

(Genesis 35:20) (...Jasher 36:11) (...Jubilees 32:34)
And Jacob set a pillar on her grave on the road above her grave: that is the pillar of Rachel's grave to this day. And the days of Rachel were forty-five years and she died.

(Genesis 35:21) (Jasher 36:13...)
And it was after the death of Rachel, Israel journeyed And spread his tent beyond the tower of Edar.

(Genesis 35:22...) (...Jasher 36:13) (Jubilees 33:1...)
And it came to pass, when Israel dwelt in that land, to the south of Magdaladra'ef, that Jacob pitched his tent in the tent of Rachel's handmaid Bilhah.

(...Jubilees 33:1)
And Jacob went to his father Isaac, he and Leah his wife, on

the new moon of the tenth month.

(Jasher 36:14)
And Reuben was jealous for his mother Leah on account of this, and he was filled with anger, and he rose up in his anger and went and entered the tent of Bilhah and he thence removed his father's bed.

(Jubilees 33:2)
And Reuben saw Bilhah, Rachel's maid, the concubine of his father, bathing in water in a secret place, and he loved her.

(Jubilees 33:3)
And he hid himself at night, and he entered the house of Bilhah at night, and he found her sleeping alone on a bed in her house.

(...Genesis 35:22...) (Jubilees 33:4)
And Reuben went and lay with Bilhah his father's concubine: and she awoke and saw, and behold Reuben was lying with her in the bed, and she uncovered the border of her covering and seized him, and cried out, and discovered that it was Reuben.

(Jubilees 33:5)
And she was ashamed because of him, and released her hand from him, and he fled.

(Jubilees 33:6)
And she lamented because of this thing exceedingly, and did not tell it to anyone.

(Jubilees 33:7)
And when Jacob returned and sought her, she said to him: I

am not clean for you, for I have been defiled as regards you; for Reuben has defiled me, and has lain with me in the night, and I was asleep, and did not discover until he uncovered my skirt and slept with me.

(...Genesis 35:22...) (Jubilees 33:8)
And Israel was exceedingly mad at Reuben when heard he had uncovered his father's skirt.

(Jasher 36:15)
At that time the portion of birthright, together with the kingly and priestly offices, was removed from the sons of Reuben, for he had profaned his father's bed, and the birthright was given to Joseph, the kingly office to Judah, and the priesthood to Levi, because Reuben had defiled his father's bed.

(Jubilees 33:9)
And Jacob did not approach her again because Reuben had defiled her. And as for any man who uncovers his father's skirt his deed is wicked exceedingly, for he is abominable before the Lord.

(Jubilees 33:10)
For this reason, it is written and ordained on the heavenly tablets that a man should not lie with his father's wife, and should not uncover his father's skirt, for this is unclean: they shall surely die together, the man who lies with his father's wife and the woman also, for they have wrought uncleanness on the earth.

(Jubilees 33:11)
And there shall be nothing unclean before our God in the nation which He has chosen for Himself as a possession.

(Jubilees 33:12)
And again, it is written a second time: Cursed be he who lies with the wife of his father, for he has uncovered his father's shame; and all the holy ones of the Lord said So be it; so be it.

(Jubilees 33:13)
And you, Moses, command the children of Israel that they observe this word; for it entails a punishment of death; and it is unclean, and there is no atonement forever to atone for the man who has committed this, but he is to be put to death and slain, and stoned with stones, and rooted out from the midst of the people of our God.

(Jubilees 33:14)
For to no man who does so in Israel is it permitted to remain alive a single day on the earth, for he is abominable and unclean.

(Jubilees 33:15)
And let them not say: to Reuben was granted life and forgiveness after he had lain with his father's concubine, and to her also though she had a husband, and her husband Jacob, his father, was still alive.

(Jubilees 33:16)
For until that time there had not been revealed the ordinance and judgment and law in its completeness for all, but in your days, it has been revealed as a law of seasons and of days, and an everlasting law for the everlasting generations.

(Jubilees 33:17)
And for this law there is no consummation of days, and no atonement for it, but they must both be rooted out in the midst of the nation: on the day whereon they committed it, they shall slay them.

(Jubilees 33:18)
And do you, Moses, write it down for Israel that they may observe it, and do according to these words, and not commit a sin to death; for the Lord our God is judge, who respects not persons and accepts not gifts.

(Jubilees 33:19)
And tell them these words of the covenant, that they may hear and observe, and be on their guard with respect to them, and not be destroyed and rooted out of the land; for an uncleanness, and an abomination, and a contamination, and a pollution are all they who commit it on the earth before our God.

(Jubilees 33:20)
And there is no greater sin than the fornication which they commit on earth; for Israel is a holy nation to the Lord its God, and a nation of inheritance, and a priestly and royal nation and for His own possession; and there shall no such uncleanness appear in the midst of the holy nation.

(Jubilees 33:21)
And in the third year of this sixth week, Jacob and all his sons went and dwelt in the house of Abraham, near Isaac his father and Rebecca his mother.

(...Genesis 35:22) (Jasher 36:16)
And these are the generations of Jacob who were born to him in Padan-aram, and the sons of Jacob were twelve.

(Genesis 35:23) (Jasher 36:17...) (Jubilees 33:22...)
And these were the names of the sons of Jacob: The sons of Leah; Reuben, Jacob's firstborn, and Simeon, and Levi, and Judah, and Issachar, and Zebulun, and their sister Dinah, the

daughter of Leah, the only daughter of Jacob.

(Genesis 35:24) (...Jasher 36:17) (...Jubilees 33:22...)
The sons of Rachel; Joseph, and Benjamin:

(Genesis 35:25) (Jasher 36:18...) (...Jubilees 33:22...)
And the sons of Bilhah, Rachel's handmaid; Dan, and Naphtali:

(Genesis 35:26) (...Jasher 36:18) (...Jubilees 33:22)
And the sons of Zilpah, Leah's handmaid; Gad, and Asher: these are the sons of Jacob, which were born to him in Padanaram.

(Jasher 37:1)
And in the one hundred and fifth year of the life of Jacob, that is the ninth year of Jacob's dwelling with his children in the land of Canaan, he came from Padan-aram.

(Genesis 35:27) (Jasher 36:19, 38...) (Jubilees 33:23)
And Jacob and his sons and all belonging to him journeyed and came to Mamre, to the city of Kireath-Arbah, which is in Hebron, where Abraham and Isaac sojourned and bowed themselves to Isaac his father and Rebecca. And when they saw them they blessed Jacob and all his sons, and Isaac rejoiced exceedingly, for he saw the sons of Jacob, his younger son and he blessed them. And Jacob with his sons and all belonging to him, dwelt with his father in Hebron, in the land of Canaan, as the Lord had commanded Abraham their father.

(Jasher 37:2)
And in those days Jacob journeyed with his children from Hebron, and they went and returned to the city of Shechem,

they and all belonging to them, and they dwelt there, for the children of Jacob obtained good and fat pasture land for their cattle in the city of Shechem, the city of Shechem having then been rebuilt, and there were in it about three hundred men and women.

(Jasher 37:3)
And Jacob and his children and all belonging to him dwelt in the part of the field which Jacob had bought from Hamor the father of Shechem, when he came from Padan-aram before Simeon and Levi had smitten the city.

(Jubilees 34:1)
And in the sixth year of this week of this forty-fourth jubilee, Jacob sent his sons to pasture their sheep, and his servants with them to the pastures of Shechem.

(Jasher 37:4)
And all those kings of the Canaanites and Amorites that surrounded the city of Shechem, heard that the sons of Jacob had again come to Shechem and dwelt there.

(Jasher 37:5)
And they said, Shall the sons of Jacob the Hebrew again come to the city and dwell therein, after that they have smitten its inhabitants and driven them out? Shall they now return and also drive out those who are dwelling in the city or slay them?

(Jasher 37:6) (Jubilees 34:2)
And all seven of the kings of the Amorites of Canaan again assembled, and they came together to make war with Jacob and his sons, to slay them, hiding themselves under the trees, and to take their cattle as a prey.

(Jubilees 34:3)
And Jacob and Levi and Judah and Joseph were in the house with Isaac their father; for his spirit was sorrowful, and they could not leave him: and Benjamin was the youngest, and for this reason remained with his father.

(Jasher 37:7)
And Jashub king of Tapnach sent also to all his neighboring kings, to Elan king of Gaash, and to Ihuri king of Shiloh, and to Parathon king of Chazar, and to Susi king of Sarton, and to Laban king of Bethchoran, and to Shabir king of Othnaymah, saying,

(Jasher 37:8)
Come up to me and assist me, and let us smite Jacob the Hebrew and his sons, and all belonging to him, for they are again come to Shechem to possess it and to slay its inhabitants as before.

(Jubilees 34:4)
And there came the kings of Taphu and the kings of Aresa, and the kings of Seragan, and the kings of Selo, and the kings of Ga'as, and the king of Bethoron, and the king of Ma'anisakir, and all those who dwell in these mountains and who dwell in the woods in the land of Canaan.

(Jasher 37:9)
And all these kings assembled together and came with all their camps, a people exceedingly plentiful like the sand upon the sea shore, and they were all opposite to Tapnach.

(Jasher 37:10)
And Jashub king of Tapnach went forth to them with all his army, and he encamped with them opposite to Tapnach

without the city, and all these kings they divided into seven divisions, being seven camps against the sons of Jacob.

(Jasher 37:11) (Jubilees 34:5)
And they announced this and they sent a declaration to Jacob and his son, saying, Come forth all of you to us that we may have an interview together in the plain, and revenge the cause of the men of Shechem whom you slew in their city, and you will now again return to the city of Shechem and dwell therein, and slay its inhabitants as before. Behold, the kings of the Amorites have surrounded your sons, and plundered their herds.

(Jasher 37:12)
And the sons of Jacob heard this and their anger was kindled exceedingly at the words of the kings of Canaan, and ten of the sons of Jacob hastened and rose up, and each of them girt on his weapons of war; and there were one hundred and two of their servants with them equipped in battle array.

(Jasher 37:13) (Jubilees 34:6)
And all these men, the sons of Jacob with their servants, went toward these kings. And Jacob arose from his house, he and his three sons and all the servants of his father, and his own servants, and he went against them with six thousand men, who carried swords. And Jacob their father was with them, and they all stood upon the heap of Shechem.

(Jasher 37:14)
And Jacob prayed to the Lord for his sons, and he spread forth his hands to the Lord, and he said, O God, you are an Almighty God, you are our father, you formed us and we are the works of your hands; I pray you deliver my sons through your mercy from the hand of their enemies, who are this day coming to fight with them and save them from their hand,

for in your hand is power and might, to save the few from the many.

(Jasher 37:15)
And give to my sons, your servants, strength of heart and might to fight with their enemies, to subdue them, and make their enemies fall before them, and let not my sons and their servants die through the hands of the children of Canaan.

(Jasher 37:16)
But if it seems good in your eyes to take away the lives of my sons and their servants, take them in your great mercy through the hands of your ministers, that they may not perish this day by the hands of the kings of the Amorites.

(Jasher 37:17)
And when Jacob ceased praying to the Lord the earth shook from its place, and the sun darkened, and all these kings were terrified and a great consternation seized them.

(Jasher 37:18)
And the Lord hearkened to the prayer of Jacob, and the Lord impressed the hearts of all the kings and their hosts with the terror and awe of the sons of Jacob.

(Jasher 37:19)
For the Lord caused them to hear the voice of chariots, and the voice of mighty horses from the sons of Jacob, and the voice of a great army accompanying them.

(Jasher 37:20)
And these kings were seized with great terror at the sons of Jacob, and while they were standing in their quarters, behold the sons of Jacob advanced upon them, with one hundred and

twelve men, with a great and tremendous shouting.

(Jasher 37:21)
And when the kings saw the sons of Jacob advancing toward them, they were still more panic struck, and they were inclined to retreat from before the sons of Jacob as at first, and not to fight with them.

(Jasher 37:22)
But they did not retreat, saying, It would be a disgrace to us thus twice to retreat from before the Hebrews.

(Jasher 37:23)
And the sons of Jacob came near and advanced against all these kings and their armies, and they saw, and behold it was a very mighty people, numerous as the sand of the sea.

(Jasher 37:24)
And the sons of Jacob called to the Lord and said, Help us O Lord, help us and answer us, for we trust in you, and let us not die by the hands of these uncircumcised men, who this day have come against us.

(Jasher 37:25)
And the sons of Jacob girt on their weapons of war, and they took in their hands each man his shield and his javelin, and they approached to battle.

(Jasher 37:26)
And Judah, the son of Jacob, ran first before his brothers, and ten of his servants with him, and he went toward these kings.

(Jasher 37:27)
And Jashub, king of Tapnach, also came forth first with his

army before Judah, and Judah saw Jashub and his army coming toward him, and Judah's wrath was kindled, and his anger burned within him, and he approached to battle in which Judah ventured his life.

(Jasher 37:28)
And Jashub and all his army were advancing toward Judah, and he was riding upon a very strong and powerful horse, and Jashub was a very valiant man, and covered with iron and brass from head to foot.

(Jasher 37:29)
And while he was upon the horse, he shot arrows with both hands from before and behind, as was his manner in all his battles, and he never missed the place to which he aimed his arrows.

(Jasher 37:30)
And when Jashub came to fight with Judah, and was darting many arrows against Judah, the Lord bound the hand of Jashub, and all the arrows that he shot rebounded upon his own men.

(Jasher 37:31)
And notwithstanding this, Jashub kept advancing toward Judah, to challenge him with the arrows, but the distance between them was about thirty cubits, and when Judah saw Jashub darting forth his arrows against him, he ran to him with his wrath-excited might.

(Jasher 37:32)
And Judah took up a large stone from the ground, and its weight was sixty shekels, and Judah ran toward Jashub, and with the stone struck him on his shield, that Jashub

was stunned with the blow, and fell off from his horse to the ground.

(Jasher 37:33)
And the shield burst asunder out of the hand of Jashub, and through the force of the blow sprang to the distance of about fifteen cubits, and the shield fell before the second camp.

(Jasher 37:34)
And the kings that came with Jashub saw at a distance the strength of Judah, the son of Jacob, and what he had done to Jashub, and they were terribly afraid of Judah.

(Jasher 37:35)
And they assembled near Jashub's camp, seeing his confusion, and Judah drew his sword and smote forty-two men of the camp of Jashub, and the whole of Jashub's camp fled before Judah, and no man stood against him, and they left Jashub and fled from him, and Jashub was still prostrate upon the ground.

(Jasher 37:36)
And Jashub seeing that all the men of his camp had fled from him, hastened and rose up with terror against Judah, and stood upon his legs opposite Judah.

(Jasher 37:37)
And Jashub had a single combat with Judah, placing shield toward shield, and Jashub's men all fled, for they were greatly afraid of Judah.

(Jasher 37:38)
And Jashub took his spear in his hand to strike Judah upon his head, but Judah had quickly placed his shield to his head

against Jashub's spear, so that the shield of Judah received the blow from Jashub's spear, and the shield was split in too.

(Jasher 37:39)
And when Judah saw that his shield was split, he hastily drew his sword and smote Jashub at his ankles, and cut off his feet that Jashub fell upon the ground, and the spear fell from his hand.

(Jasher 37:40)
And Judah hastily picked up Jashub's spear, with which he severed his head and cast it next to his feet.

(Jasher 37:41)
And when the sons of Jacob saw what Judah had done to Jashub, they all ran into the ranks of the other kings, and the sons of Jacob fought with the army of Jashub, and the armies of all the kings that were there.

(Jasher 37:42)
And the sons of Jacob caused fifteen thousand of their men to fall, and they smote them as if smiting at gourds, and the rest fled for their lives.

(Jasher 37:43)
And Judah was still standing by the body of Jashub, and stripped Jashub of his coat of mail.

(Jasher 37:44)
And Judah also took off the iron and brass that was about Jashub, and behold nine men of the captains of Jashub came along to fight against Judah.

(Jasher 37:45)
And Judah hastened and took up a stone from the ground, and with it smote one of them upon the head, and his skull was fractured, and the body also fell from the horse to the ground.

(Jasher 37:46)
And the eight captains that remained, seeing the strength of Judah, were greatly afraid and they fled, and Judah with his ten men pursued them, and they overtook them and slew them.

(Jasher 37:47)
And the sons of Jacob were still smiting the armies of the kings, and they slew many of them, but those kings daringly kept their stand with their captains, and did not retreat from their places, and they exclaimed against those of their armies that fled from before the sons of Jacob, but none would listen to them, for they were afraid of their lives lest they should die.

(Jasher 37:48)
And all the sons of Jacob, after having smitten the armies of the kings, returned and came before Judah, and Judah was still slaying the eight captains of Jashub, and stripping off their garments.

(Jasher 37:49)
And Levi saw Elon, king of Gaash, advancing toward him, with his fourteen captains to smite him, but Levi did not know it for certain.

(Jasher 37:50)
And Elon with his captains approached nearer, and Levi looked back and saw that battle was given him in the rear, and

Levi ran with twelve of his servants, and they went and slew Elon and his captains with the edge of the sword.

~ ~ ~

(Jasher 38:1)
And Ihuri king of Shiloh came up to assist Elon, and he approached Jacob, when Jacob drew his bow that was in his hand and with an arrow struck Ihuri which caused his death.

(Jasher 38:2)
And when Ihuri king of Shiloh was dead, the four remaining kings fled from their station with the rest of the captains, and they endeavored to retreat, saying, We have no more strength with the Hebrews after their having killed the three kings and their captains who were more powerful than we are.

(Jasher 38:3)
And when the sons of Jacob saw that the remaining kings had removed from their station, they pursued them, and Jacob also came from the heap of Shechem from the place where he was standing, and they went after the kings and they approached them with their servants.

(Jasher 38:4)
And the kings and the captains with the rest of their armies, seeing that the sons of Jacob approached them, were afraid of their lives and fled till they reached the city of Chazar.

(Jasher 38:5)
And the sons of Jacob pursued them to the gate of the city of Chazar, and they smote a great smiting among the kings and

their armies, about four thousand men, and while they were smiting the army of the kings, Jacob was occupied with his bow confining himself to smiting the kings, and he slew them all.

(Jasher 38:6)
And he slew Parathon king of Chazar at the gate of the city of Chazar, and he afterward smote Susi king of Sarton, and Laban king of Bethchorin, and Shabir king of Machnaymah, and he slew them all with arrows, an arrow to each of them, and they died.

(Jasher 38:7)
And the sons of Jacob seeing that all the kings were dead and that they were broken up and retreating, continued to carry on the battle with the armies of the kings opposite the gate of Chazar, and they still smote about four hundred of their men.

(Jasher 38:8)
And three men of the servants of Jacob fell in that battle, and when Judah saw that three of his servants had died, it grieved him greatly, and his anger burned within him against the Amorites.

(Jasher 38:9)
And all the men that remained of the armies of the kings were greatly afraid of their lives, and they ran and broke the gate of the walls of the city of Chazar, and they all entered the city for safety.

(Jasher 38:10)
And they concealed themselves in the midst of the city of Chazar, for the city of Chazar was very large and extensive, and when all these armies had entered the city, the sons of

Jacob ran after them to the city.

(Jasher 38:11)
And four mighty men, experienced in battle, went forth from the city and stood against the entrance of the city, with drawn swords and spears in their hands, and they placed themselves opposite the sons of Jacob, and would not suffer them to enter the city.

(Jasher 38:12)
And Naphtali ran and came between them and with his sword smote two of them, and cut off their heads at one stroke.

(Jasher 38:13)
And he turned to the other two, and behold they had fled, and he pursued them, overtook them, smote them and slew them.

(Jasher 38:14)
And the sons of Jacob came to the city and saw, and behold there was another wall to the city, and they sought for the gate of the wall and could not find it, and Judah sprang upon the top of the wall, and Simeon and Levi followed him, and they all three descended from the wall into the city.

(Jasher 38:15)
And Simeon and Levi slew all the men who ran for safety into the city, and also the inhabitants of the city with their wives and little ones, they slew with the edge of the sword, and the cries of the city ascended up to heaven.

(Jasher 38:16)
And Dan and Naphtali sprang upon the wall to see what caused the noise of lamentation, for the sons of Jacob felt anxious about their brothers, and they heard the inhabitants

of the city speaking with weeping and supplications, saying, Take all that we possess in the city and go away, only do not put us to death.

(Jasher 38:17)
And when Judah, Simeon, and Levi had ceased smiting the inhabitants of the city, they ascended the wall and called to Dan and Naphtali, who were upon the wall, and to the rest of their brothers, and Simeon and Levi informed them of the entrance into the city, and all the sons of Jacob came to fetch the spoil.

(Jasher 38:18)
And the sons of Jacob took the spoil of the city of Chazar, the flocks and herds, and the property, and they took all that could be captured, and went away that day from the city.

(Jasher 38:19)
And on the next day the sons of Jacob went to Sarton, for they heard that the men of Sarton who had remained in the city were assembling to fight with them for having slain their king, and Sarton was a very high and fortified city, and it had a deep rampart surrounding the city.

(Jasher 38:20)
And the pillar of the rampart was about fifty cubits and its breadth forty cubits, and there was no place for a man to enter the city on account of the rampart, and the sons of Jacob saw the rampart of the city, and they sought an entrance in it but could not find it.

(Jasher 38:21)
For the entrance to the city was at the rear, and every man that wished to come into the city came by that road and went

around the whole city, and he afterwards entered the city.

(Jasher 38:22)
And the sons of Jacob seeing they could not find the way into the city, their anger was kindled greatly, and the inhabitants of the city seeing that the sons of Jacob were coming to them were greatly afraid of them, for they had heard of their strength and what they had done to Chazar.

(Jasher 38:23)
And the inhabitants of the city of Sarton could not go out toward the sons of Jacob after having assembled in the city to fight against them, lest they might thereby get into the city, but when they saw that they were coming toward them, they were greatly afraid of them, for they had heard of their strength and what they had done to Chazar.

(Jasher 38:24)
So the inhabitants of Sarton speedily took away the bridge of the road of the city, from its place, before the sons of Jacob came, and they brought it into the city.

(Jasher 38:25)
And the sons of Jacob came and sought the way into the city, and could not find it and the inhabitants of the city went up to the top of the wall, and saw, and behold the sons of Jacob were seeking an entrance into the city.

(Jasher 38:26)
And the inhabitants of the city reproached the sons of Jacob from the top of the wall, and they cursed them, and the sons of Jacob heard the reproaches, and they were greatly incensed, and their anger burned within them.

(Jasher 38:27)
And the sons of Jacob were provoked at them, and they all rose and sprang over the rampart with the force of their strength, and through their might passed the forty cubits' breadth of the rampart.

(Jasher 38:28)
And when they had passed the rampart they stood under the wall of the city, and they found all the gates of the city enclosed with iron doors.

(Jasher 38:29)
And the sons of Jacob came near to break open the doors of the gates of the city, and the inhabitants did not let them, for from the top of the wall they were casting stones and arrows upon them.

(Jasher 38:30)
And the number of the people that were upon the wall was about four hundred men, and when the sons of Jacob saw that the men of the city would not let them open the gates of the city, they sprang and ascended the top of the wall, and Judah went up first to the east part of the city.

(Jasher 38:31)
And Gad and Asher went up after him to the west corner of the city, and Simeon and Levi to the north, and Dan and Reuben to the south.

(Jasher 38:32)
And the men who were on the top of the wall, the inhabitants of the city, seeing that the sons of Jacob were coming up to them, they all fled from the wall, descended into the city, and concealed themselves in the midst of the city.

(Jasher 38:33)
And Issachar and Naphtali that remained under the wall approached and broke the gates of the city, and kindled a fire at the gates of the city, that the iron melted, and all the sons of Jacob came into the city, they and all their men, and they fought with the inhabitants of the city of Sarton, and smote them with the edge of the sword, and no man stood up before them.

(Jasher 38:34)
And about two hundred men fled from the city, and they all went and hid themselves in a certain tower in the city, and Judah pursued them to the tower and he broke down the tower, which fell upon the men, and they all died.

(Jasher 38:35)
And the sons of Jacob went up the road of the roof of that tower, and they saw, and behold there was another strong and high tower at a distance in the city, and the top of it reached to heaven, and the sons of Jacob hastened and descended, and went with all their men to that tower, and found it filled with about three hundred men, women and little ones.

(Jasher 38:36)
And the sons of Jacob smote a great smiting among those men in the tower and they ran away and fled from them.

(Jasher 38:37)
And Simeon and Levi pursued them, when twelve mighty and valiant men came out to them from the place where they had concealed themselves.

(Jasher 38:38)
And those twelve men maintained a strong battle against

Simeon and Levi, and Simeon and Levi could not prevail over them, and those valiant men broke the shields of Simeon and Levi, and one of them struck at Levi's head with his sword, when Levi hastily placed his hand to his head, for he was afraid of the sword, and the sword struck Levi's hand, and it wanted but little to the hand of Levi being cut off.

(Jasher 38:39)
And Levi seized the sword of the valiant man in his hand, and took it forcibly from the man, and with it he struck at the head of the powerful man, and he severed his head.

(Jasher 38:40)
And eleven men approached to fight with Levi, for they saw that one of them was killed, and the sons of Jacob fought, but the sons of Jacob could not prevail over them, for those men were very powerful.

(Jasher 38:41)
And the sons of Jacob seeing that they could not prevail over them, Simeon gave a loud and tremendous shriek, and the eleven powerful men were stunned at the voice of Simeon's shrieking.

(Jasher 38:42)
And Judah at a distance knew the voice of Simeon's shouting, and Naphtali and Judah ran with their shields to Simeon and Levi, and found them fighting with those powerful men, unable to prevail over them as their shields were broken.

(Jasher 38:43)
And Naphtali saw that the shields of Simeon and Levi were broken, and he took two shields from his servants and brought them to Simeon and Levi.

(Jasher 38:44)
And Simeon, Levi and Judah on that day fought all three against the eleven mighty men until the time of sunset, but they could not prevail over them.

(Jasher 38:45)
And this was told to Jacob, and he was sorely grieved, and he prayed to the Lord, and he and Naphtali his son went against these mighty men.

(Jasher 38:46)
And Jacob approached and drew his bow, and came nigh to the mighty men, and slew three of their men with the bow, and the remaining eight turned back, and behold, the war waged against them in the front and rear, and they were greatly afraid of their lives, and could not stand before the sons of Jacob, and they fled from before them.

(Jasher 38:47)
And in their flight, they met Dan and Asher coming toward them, and they suddenly fell upon them, and fought with them, and slew two of them, and Judah and his brothers pursued them, and smote the remainder of them, and slew them.

(Jasher 38:48)
And all the sons of Jacob returned and walked about the city, searching if they could find any men, and they found about twenty young men in a cave in the city, and Gad and Asher smote them all, and Dan and Naphtali lighted upon the rest of the men who had fled and escaped from the second tower, and they smote them all.

(Jasher 38:49)
And the sons of Jacob smote all the inhabitants of the city of Sarton, but the women and little ones they left in the city and did not slay them.

(Jasher 38:50)
And all the inhabitants of the city of Sarton were powerful men, one of them would pursue a thousand, and two of them would not flee from ten thousand of the rest of men.

(Jasher 38:51)
And the sons of Jacob slew all the inhabitants of the city of Sarton with the edge of the sword, that no man stood up against them, and they left the women in the city.

(Jasher 38:52)
And the sons of Jacob took all the spoil of the city, and captured what they desired, and they took flocks and herds and property from the city, and the sons of Jacob did to Sarton and its inhabitants as they had done to Chazar and its inhabitants, and they turned and went away.

~ ~ ~

(Jasher 39:1)
And when the sons of Jacob went from the city of Sarton, they had gone about two hundred cubits when they met the inhabitants of Tapnach coming toward them, for they went out to fight with them, because they had smitten the king of Tapnach and all his men.

(Jasher 39:2)
So all that remained in the city of Tapnach came out to fight with the sons of Jacob, and they thought to retake from them the booty and the spoil which they had captured from Chazar and Sarton.

(Jasher 39:3)
And the rest of the men of Tapnach fought with the sons of Jacob in that place, and the sons of Jacob smote them, and they fled before them, and they pursued them to the city of Arbelan, and they all fell before the sons of Jacob.

(Jasher 39:4)
And the sons of Jacob returned and came to Tapnach, to take away the spoil of Tapnach, and when they came to Tapnach they heard that the people of Arbelan had gone out to meet them to save the spoil of their brothers, and the sons of Jacob left ten of their men in Tapnach to plunder the city, and they went out toward the people of Arbelan.

(Jasher 39:5)
And the men of Arbelan went out with their wives to fight with the sons of Jacob, for their wives were experienced in battle, and they went out, about four hundred men and women.

(Jasher 39:6)
And all the sons of Jacob shouted with a loud voice, and they all ran toward the inhabitants of Arbelan, and with a great and tremendous voice.

(Jasher 39:7)
And the inhabitants of Arbelan heard the noise of the shouting of the sons of Jacob, and their roaring like the noise of lions and like the roaring of the sea and its waves.

(Jasher 39:8)
And fear and terror possessed their hearts on account of the sons of Jacob, and they were terribly afraid of them, and they retreated and fled before them into the city, and the sons of Jacob pursued them to the gate of the city, and they came upon them in the city.

(Jasher 39:9)
And the sons of Jacob fought with them in the city, and all their women were engaged in slinging against the sons of Jacob, and the combat was very severe among them the whole of that day till evening.

(Jasher 39:10)
And the sons of Jacob could not prevail over them, and the sons of Jacob had almost perished in that battle, and the sons of Jacob cried to the Lord and greatly gained strength toward evening, and the sons of Jacob smote all the inhabitants of Arbelan by the edge of the sword, men, women and little ones.

(Jasher 39:11)
And also, the remainder of the people who had fled from Sarton, the sons of Jacob smote them in Arbelan, and the sons of Jacob did to Arbelan and Tapnach as they had done to Chazar and Sarton, and when the women saw that all the men were dead, they went upon the roofs of the city and smote the sons of Jacob by showering down stones like rain.

(Jasher 39:12)
And the sons of Jacob hastened and came into the city and seized all the women and smote them with the edge of the sword, and the sons of Jacob captured all the spoil and booty, flocks and herds and cattle.

(Jasher 39:13)
And the sons of Jacob did to Machnaymah as they had done to Tapnach, to Chazar and to Shiloh, and they turned from there and went away.

(Jasher 39:14)
And on the fifth day the sons of Jacob heard that the people of Gaash had gathered against them to battle, because they had slain their king and their captains, for there had been fourteen captains in the city of Gaash, and the sons of Jacob had slain them all in the first battle.

(Jasher 39:15)
And the sons of Jacob that day girt on their weapons of war, and they marched to battle against the inhabitants of Gaash, and in Gaash there was a strong and mighty people of the people of the Amorites, and Gaash was the strongest and best fortified city of all the cities of the Amorites, and it had three walls.

(Jasher 39:16)
And the sons of Jacob came to Gaash and they found the gates of the city locked, and about five hundred men standing at the top of the outer-most wall, and a people numerous as the sand upon the sea shore were in ambush for the sons of Jacob from without the city at the rear thereof.

(Jasher 39:17)
And the sons of Jacob approached to open the gates of the city, and while they were drawing nigh, behold those who were in ambush at the rear of the city came forth from their places and surrounded the sons of Jacob.

(Jasher 39:18)
And the sons of Jacob were enclosed between the people of Gaash, and the battle was both to their front and rear, and all the men that were upon the wall, were casting from the wall upon them, arrows and stones.

(Jasher 39:19)
And Judah, seeing that the men of Gaash were getting too heavy for them, gave a most piercing and tremendous shriek and all the men of Gaash were terrified at the voice of Judah's cry, and men fell from the wall at his powerful shriek, and all those that were from without and within the city were greatly afraid of their lives.

(Jasher 39:20)
And the sons of Jacob still came nigh to break the doors of the city, when the men of Gaash threw stones and arrows upon them from the top of the wall, and made them flee from the gate.

(Jasher 39:21)
And the sons of Jacob returned against the men of Gaash who were with them from without the city, and they smote them terribly, as striking against gourds, and they could not stand against the sons of Jacob, for fright and terror had seized them at the shriek of Judah.

(Jasher 39:22)
And the sons of Jacob slew all those men who were without the city, and the sons of Jacob still drew nigh to effect an entrance into the city, and to fight under the city walls, but they could not for all the inhabitants of Gaash who remained in the city had surrounded the walls of Gaash in every direction, so that the sons of Jacob were unable to approach the city to fight with them.

(Jasher 39:23)
And the sons of Jacob came nigh to one corner to fight under the wall, the inhabitants of Gaash threw arrows and stones upon them like showers of rain, and they fled from under the wall.

(Jasher 39:24)
And the people of Gaash who were upon the wall, seeing that the sons of Jacob could not prevail over them from under the wall, reproached the sons of Jacob in these words, saying,

(Jasher 39:25)
What is the matter with you in the battle that you cannot prevail? Can you then do to the mighty city of Gaash and its inhabitants as you did to the cities of the Amorites that were not so powerful? Surely to those weak ones among us you did those things, and slew them in the entrance of the city, for they had no strength when they were terrified at the sound of your shouting.

(Jasher 39:26)
And will you now then be able to fight in this place? Surely here you will all die, and we will avenge the cause of those cities that you have laid waste.

(Jasher 39:27)
And the inhabitants of Gaash greatly reproached the sons of Jacob and reviled them with their gods, and continued to cast arrows and stones upon them from the wall.

(Jasher 39:28)
And Judah and his brothers heard the words of the inhabitants of Gaash and their anger was greatly roused, and Judah was jealous of his God in this matter, and he called out and said, O

Lord, help, send help to us and our brothers.

(Jasher 39:29)
And he ran at a distance with all his might, with his drawn sword in his hand, and he sprang from the earth and by dint of his strength, mounted the wall, and his sword fell from his hand.

(Jasher 39:30)
And Judah shouted upon the wall, and all the men that were upon the wall were terrified, and some of them fell from the wall into the city and died, and those who were yet upon the wall, when they saw Judah's strength, they were greatly afraid and fled for their lives into the city for safety.

(Jasher 39:31)
And some were emboldened to fight with Judah upon the wall, and they came nigh to slay him when they saw there was no sword in Judah's hand, and they thought of casting him from the wall to his brothers, and twenty men of the city came up to assist them, and they surrounded Judah and they all shouted over him, and approached him with drawn swords, and they terrified Judah, and Judah cried out to his brothers from the wall.

(Jasher 39:32)
And Jacob and his sons drew the bow from under the wall, and smote three of the men that were upon the top of the wall, and Judah continued to cry and he exclaimed, O Lord help us, O Lord deliver us, and he cried out with a loud voice upon the wall, and the cry was heard at a great distance.

(Jasher 39:33)
And after this cry he again repeated to shout, and all the men

who surrounded Judah on the top of the wall were terrified, and they each threw his sword from his hand at the sound of Judah's shouting and his tremor, and fled.

(Jasher 39:34)
And Judah took the swords which had fallen from their hands, and Judah fought with them and slew twenty of their men upon the wall.

(Jasher 39:35)
And about eighty men and women still ascended the wall from the city and they all surrounded Judah, and the Lord impressed the fear of Judah in their hearts, that they were unable to approach him.

(Jasher 39:36)
And Jacob and all who were with him drew the bow from under the wall, and they slew ten men upon the wall, and they fell below the wall, before Jacob and his sons.

(Jasher 39:37)
And the people upon the wall seeing that twenty of their men had fallen, they still ran toward Judah with drawn swords, but they could not approach him for they were greatly terrified at Judah's strength.

(Jasher 39:38)
And one of their mighty men whose name was Arud approached to strike Judah upon the head with his sword, when Judah hastily put his shield to his head, and the sword hit the shield, and it was split in two.

(Jasher 39:39)
And this mighty man after he had struck Judah ran for his

life, at the fear of Judah, and his feet slipped upon the wall and he fell among the sons of Jacob who were below the wall, and the sons of Jacob smote him and slew him.

(Jasher 39:40)
And Judah's head pained him from the blow of the powerful man, and Judah had nearly died from it.

(Jasher 39:41)
And Judah cried out upon the wall owing to the pain produced by the blow, when Dan heard him, and his anger burned within him, and he also rose up and went at a distance and ran and sprang from the earth and mounted the wall with his wrath-excited strength.

(Jasher 39:42)
And when Dan came upon the wall near to Judah all the men upon the wall fled, who had stood against Judah, and they went up to the second wall, and they threw arrows and stones upon Dan and Judah from the second wall, and endeavored to drive them from the wall.

(Jasher 39:43)
And the arrows and stones struck Dan and Judah, and they had nearly been killed upon the wall, and wherever Dan and Judah fled from the wall, they were attacked with arrows and stones from the second wall.

(Jasher 39:44)
And Jacob and his sons were still at the entrance of the city below the first wall, and they were not able to draw their bow against the inhabitants of the city, as they could not be seen by them, being upon the second wall.

(Jasher 39:45)
And Dan and Judah when they could no longer bear the stones and arrows that fell upon them from the second wall, they both sprang upon the second wall near the people of the city, and when the people of the city who were upon the second wall saw that Dan and Judah had come to them upon the second wall, they all cried out and descended below between the walls.

(Jasher 39:46)
And Jacob and his sons heard the noise of the shouting from the people of the city, and they were still at the entrance of the city, and they were anxious about Dan and Judah who were not seen by them, for they were upon the second wall.

(Jasher 39:47)
And Naphtali went up with his wrath-excited might and sprang upon the first wall to see what caused the noise of shouting which they had heard in the city, and Issachar and Zebulun drew nigh to break the doors of the city, and they opened the gates of the city and came into the city.

(Jasher 39:48)
And Naphtali leaped from the first wall to the second, and came to assist his brothers, and the inhabitants of Gaash who were upon the wall, seeing that Naphtali was the third who had come up to assist his brothers, they all fled and descended into the city, and Jacob and all his sons and all their young men came into the city to them.

(Jasher 39:49)
And Judah and Dan and Naphtali descended from the wall into the city and pursued the inhabitants of the city, and Simeon and Levi were from without the city and knew not that the gate was opened, and they went up from there to the

wall and came down to their brothers into the city.

(Jasher 39:50)
And the inhabitants of the city had all descended into the city, and the sons of Jacob came to them in different directions, and the battle waged against them from the front and the rear, and the sons of Jacob smote them terribly, and slew about twenty thousand of them men and women, not one of them could stand up against the sons of Jacob.

(Jasher 39:51)
And the blood flowed plentifully in the city, and it was like a brook of water, and the blood flowed like a brook to the outer part of the city, and reached the desert of Bethchorin.

(Jasher 39:52)
And the people of Bethchorin saw at a distance the blood flowing from the city of Gaash, and about seventy men from among them ran to see the blood, and they came to the place where the blood was.

(Jasher 39:53)
And they followed the track of the blood and came to the wall of the city of Gaash, and they saw the blood issue from the city, and they heard the voice of crying from the inhabitants of Gaash, for it ascended to heaven, and the blood was continuing to flow abundantly like a brook of water.

(Jasher 39:54)
And all the sons of Jacob were still smiting the inhabitants of Gaash, and were engaged in slaying them till evening, about twenty thousand men and women, and the people of Chorin said, Surely, this is the work of the Hebrews, for they are still carrying on war in all the cities of the Amorites.

(Jasher 39:55)
And those people hastened and ran to Bethchorin, and each took his weapons of war, and they cried out to all the inhabitants of Bethchorin, who also girt on their weapons of war to go and fight with the sons of Jacob.

(Jasher 39:56)
And when the sons of Jacob had done smiting the inhabitants of Gaash, they walked about the city to strip all the slain, and coming in the innermost part of the city and farther on they met three very powerful men, and there was no sword in their hand.

(Jasher 39:57)
And the sons of Jacob came up to the place where they were, and the powerful men ran away, and one of them had taken Zebulun, who he saw was a young lad and of short stature, and with his might dashed him to the ground.

(Jasher 39:58)
And Jacob ran to him with his sword and Jacob smote him below his loins with the sword, and cut him in two, and the body fell upon Zebulun.

(Jasher 39:59)
And the second one approached and seized Jacob to make him fall to the ground, and Jacob turned to him and shouted to him, while Simeon and Levi ran and smote him on the hips with the sword and felled him to the ground.

(Jasher 39:60)
And the powerful man rose up from the ground with wrath-excited might, and Judah came to him before he had gained his footing, and struck him upon the head with the sword, and

his head was split and he died.

(Jasher 39:61)
And the third powerful man, seeing that his companions were killed, ran from before the sons of Jacob, and the sons of Jacob pursued him in the city; and while the powerful man was fleeing he found one of the swords of the inhabitants of the city, and he picked it up and turned to the sons of Jacob and fought them with that sword.

(Jasher 39:62)
And the powerful man ran to Judah to strike him upon the head with the sword, and there was no shield in the hand of Judah; and while he was aiming to strike him, Naphtali hastily took his shield and put it to Judah's head, and the sword of the powerful man hit the shield of Naphtali and Judah escaped the sword.

(Jasher 39:63)
And Simeon and Levi ran upon the powerful man with their swords and struck at him forcibly with their swords, and the two swords entered the body of the powerful man and divided it in two, length-wise.

(Jasher 39:64)
And the sons of Jacob smote the three mighty men at that time, together with all the inhabitants of Gaash, and the day was about to decline.

(Jasher 39:65)
And the sons of Jacob walked about Gaash and took all the spoil of the city, even the little ones and women they did not suffer to live, and the sons of Jacob did to Gaash as they had done to Sarton and Shiloh.

~ ~ ~

(Jasher 40:1)
And the sons of Jacob led away all the spoil of Gaash, and went out of the city by night.

(Jasher 40:2)
They were going out marching toward the castle of Bethchorin, and the inhabitants of Bethchorin were going to the castle to meet them, and on that night the sons of Jacob fought with the inhabitants of Bethchorin, in the castle of Bethchorin.

(Jasher 40:3)
And all the inhabitants of Bethchorin were mighty men, one of them would not flee from before a thousand men, and they fought on that night upon the castle, and their shouts were heard on that night from afar, and the earth quaked at their shouting.

(Jasher 40:4)
And all the sons of Jacob were afraid of those men, as they were not accustomed to fight in the dark, and they were greatly confounded, and the sons of Jacob cried to the Lord, saying, Give help to us O Lord, deliver us that we may not die by the hands of these uncircumcised men.

(Jasher 40:5)
And the Lord hearkened to the voice of the sons of Jacob, and the Lord caused great terror and confusion to seize the people of Bethchorin, and they fought among themselves the one with the other in the darkness of night, and smote each other in great numbers.

(Jasher 40:6)
And the sons of Jacob, knowing that the Lord had brought a spirit of perverseness among those men, and that they fought each man with his neighbor, went forth from among the bands of the people of Bethchorin and went as far as the descent of the castle of Bethchorin, and farther, and they tarried there securely with their young men on that night.

(Jasher 40:7)
And the people of Bethchorin fought the whole night, one man with his brother, and the other with his neighbor, and they cried out in every direction upon the castle, and their cry was heard at a distance, and the whole earth shook at their voice, for they were powerful above all the people of the earth.

(Jasher 40:8)
And all the inhabitants of the cities of the Canaanites, the Hittites, the Amorites, the Hivites and all the kings of Canaan, and also those who were on the other side of the Jordan, heard the noise of the shouting on that night.

(Jasher 40:9)
And they said, Surely these are the battles of the Hebrews who are fighting against the seven cities, who came nigh to them; and who can stand against those Hebrews?

(Jasher 40:10)
And all the inhabitants of the cities of the Canaanites, and all those who were on the other side of the Jordan, were greatly afraid of the sons of Jacob, for they said, Behold the same will be done to us as was done to those cities, for who can stand against their mighty strength?

(Jasher 40:11)
And the cries of the Chorinites were very great on that night, and continued to increase; and they smote each other till morning, and numbers of them were killed.

(Jasher 40:12)
And the morning appeared, and all the sons of Jacob rose up at daybreak and went up to the castle, and they smote those who remained of the Chorinites in a terrible manner, and they were all killed in the castle.

(Jasher 40:13)
And the sixth day appeared, and all the inhabitants of Canaan saw at a distance all the people of Bethchorin lying dead in the castle of Bethchorin, and strewed about as the carcasses of lambs and goats.

(Jasher 40:14)
And the sons of Jacob led all the spoil which they had captured from Gaash and went to Bethchorin, and they found the city full of people like the sand of the sea, and they fought with them, and the sons of Jacob smote them there till evening time.

(Jasher 40:15)
And the sons of Jacob did to Bethchorin as they had done to Gaash and Tapnach, and as they had done to Chazar, to Sarton and to Shiloh.

(Jubilees 34:7)
And Jacob slew them in the pastures of Shechem, and pursued those who fled, and he slew them with the edge of the sword, and he slew Aresa and Taphu and Saregan and Selo and Amani-sakir and Gaga'as, and he recovered his herds.

(Jasher 40:16)
And the sons of Jacob took with them the spoil of Bethchorin and all the spoil of the cities, and on that day, they went home to Shechem.

(Jasher 40:17)
And the sons of Jacob came home to the city of Shechem, and they remained without the city, and they then rested there from the war, and tarried there all night.

(Jasher 40:18)
And all their servants together with all the spoil that they had taken from the cities, they left without the city, and they did not enter the city, for they said, Peradventure there may be yet more fighting against us, and they may come to besiege us in Shechem.

(Jasher 40:19)
And Jacob and his sons and their servants remained on that night and the next day in the portion of the field which Jacob had purchased from Hamor for five shekels, and all that they had captured was with them.

(Jasher 40:20)
And all the booty which the sons of Jacob had captured, was in the portion of the field, immense as the sand upon the sea shore.

(Jasher 40:21)
And the inhabitants of the land observed them from afar, and all the inhabitants of the land were afraid of the sons of Jacob who had done this thing, for no king from the days of old had ever done the like.

(Jasher 40:22)
And the seven kings of the Canaanites resolved to make peace with the sons of Jacob, for they were greatly afraid of their lives, on account of the sons of Jacob.

(Jasher 40:23)
And on that day, being the seventh day, Japhia king of Hebron sent secretly to the king of Ai, and to the king of Gibeon, and to the king of Shalem, and to the king of Adulam, and to the king of Lachish, and to the king of Chazar, and to all the Canaanite kings who were under their subjection, saying,

(Jasher 40:24)
Go up with me, and come to me that we may go to the sons of Jacob, and I will make peace with them, and form a treaty with them, lest all your lands be destroyed by the swords of the sons of Jacob, as they did to Shechem and the cities around it, as you have heard and seen.

(Jasher 40:25)
And when you come to me, do not come with many men, but let every king bring his three head captains, and every captain bring three of his officers.

(Jasher 40:26)
And come all of you to Hebron, and we will go together to the sons of Jacob, and supplicate them that they shall form a treaty of peace with us.

(Jasher 40:27)
And all those kings did as the king of Hebron had sent to them, for they were all under his counsel and command, and all the kings of Canaan assembled to go to the sons of Jacob, to make peace with them; and the sons of Jacob returned and

went to the portion of the field that was in Shechem, for they did not put confidence in the kings of the land.

(Jasher 40:28)
And the sons of Jacob returned and remained in the portion of the field ten days, and no one came to make war with them.

(Jasher 40:29)
And when the sons of Jacob saw that there was no appearance of war, they all assembled and went to the city of Shechem, and the sons of Jacob remained in Shechem.

(Jasher 40:30)
And at the expiration of forty days, all the kings of the Amorites assembled from all their places and came to Hebron, to Japhia, king of Hebron.

(Jasher 40:31)
And the number of kings that came to Hebron, to make peace with the sons of Jacob, was twenty-one kings, and the number of captains that came with them was sixty-nine, and their men were one hundred and eighty-nine, and all these kings and their men rested by Mount Hebron.

(Jasher 40:32)
And the king of Hebron went out with his three captains and nine men, and these kings resolved to go to the sons of Jacob to make peace.

(Jasher 40:33)
And they said to the king of Hebron, You go before us with your men, and speak for us to the sons of Jacob, and we will come after you and confirm your words, and the king of Hebron did so.

(Jasher 40:34)
And the sons of Jacob heard that all the kings of Canaan had gathered together and rested in Hebron, and the sons of Jacob sent four of their servants as spies, saying, Go and spy these kings, and search and examine their men whether they are few or many, and if they are but few in number, number them all and come back.

(Jasher 40:35)
And the servants of Jacob went secretly to these kings, and did as the sons of Jacob had commanded them, and on that day they came back to the sons of Jacob, and said to them, We came to those kings, and they are but few in number, and we numbered them all, and behold, they were two hundred and eighty-eight, kings and men.

(Jasher 40:36)
And the sons of Jacob said, They are but few in number, therefore we will not all go out to them; and in the morning the sons of Jacob rose up and chose sixty two of their men, and ten of the sons of Jacob went with them; and they girt on their weapons of war, for they said, They are coming to make war with us, for they knew not that they were coming to make peace with them.

(Jasher 40:37)
And the sons of Jacob went with their servants to the gate of Shechem, toward those kings, and their father Jacob was with them.

(Jasher 40:38)
And when they had come forth, behold, the king of Hebron and his three captains and nine men with him were coming along the road against the sons of Jacob, and the sons of Jacob

lifted up their eyes, and saw at a distance Japhia, king of Hebron, with his captains, coming toward them, and the sons of Jacob took their stand at the place of the gate of Shechem, and did not proceed.

(Jasher 40:39)
And the king of Hebron continued to advance, he and his captains, until he came nigh to the sons of Jacob, and he and his captains bowed down to them to the ground, and the king of Hebron sat with his captains before Jacob and his sons.

(Jasher 40:40)
And the sons of Jacob said to him, What has befallen you, O king of Hebron? Why have you come to us this day? What do you require from us? And the king of Hebron said to Jacob, I beseech you my lord, all the kings of the Canaanites have this day come to make peace with you.

(Jasher 40:41)
And the sons of Jacob heard the words of the king of Hebron, and they would not consent to his proposals, for the sons of Jacob had no faith in him, for they imagined that the king of Hebron had spoken deceitfully to them.

(Jasher 40:42)
And the king of Hebron knew from the words of the sons of Jacob, that they did not believe his words, and the king of Hebron approached nearer to Jacob, and said to him, I beseech you, my lord, to be assured that all these kings have come to you on peaceable terms, for they have not come with all their men, neither did they bring their weapons of war with them, for they have come to seek peace from my lord and his sons.

(Jasher 40:43)
And the sons of Jacob answered the king of Hebron, saying, Send to all these kings, and if you speak truth to us, let them each come singly before us, and if they come to us unarmed, we shall then know that they seek peace from us.

(Jasher 40:44)
And Japhia, king of Hebron, sent one of his men to the kings, and they all came before the sons of Jacob, and bowed down to them to the ground, and these kings sat before Jacob and his sons, and they spoke to them, saying,

(Jasher 40:45)
We have heard all that you did to the kings of the Amorites with your sword and exceedingly mighty arm, so that no man could stand up before you, and we were afraid of you for the sake of our lives, lest it should befall us as it did to them.

(Jasher 40:46)
So we have come to you to form a treaty of peace between us, and now therefore contract with us a covenant of peace and truth, that you will not meddle with us, inasmuch as we have not meddled with you.

(Jasher 40:47)
And the sons of Jacob knew that they had really come to seek peace from them, and the sons of Jacob listened to them, and formed a covenant with them.

(Jasher 40:48)
And the sons of Jacob swore to them that they would not meddle with them, and all the kings of the Canaanites swore also to them, and the sons of Jacob made them tributary from that day forward.

(Jubilees 34:8)
And Jacob prevailed over them, and imposed tribute on them that they should pay him tribute, five fruit products of their land, and he built Robel and Tamnatares.

(Jasher 40:49)
And after this all the captains of these kings came with their men before Jacob, with presents in their hands for Jacob and his sons, and they bowed down to him to the ground.

(Jasher 40:50)
And these kings then urged the sons of Jacob and begged of them to return all the spoil they had captured from the seven cities of the Amorites, and the sons of Jacob did so, and they returned all that they had captured, the women, the little ones, the cattle and all the spoil which they had taken, and they sent them off, and they went away each to his city.

(Jasher 40:51)
And all these kings again bowed down to the sons of Jacob, and they sent or brought them many gifts in those days, and the sons of Jacob sent off these kings and their men, and they went peaceably away from them to their cities, and the sons of Jacob also returned to their home, to Shechem.

(Jubilees 34:9)
And Jacob returned in peace, and made peace with them, and they became his servants, until the day that he and his sons went down into Egypt.

(Jasher 40:52)
And there was peace from that day forward between the sons of Jacob and the kings of the Canaanites, until the children of Israel came to inherit the land of Canaan.

~ ~ ~

(Jasher 41:1)
And at the revolution of the year the sons of Jacob journeyed from Shechem, and they came to Hebron, to their father Isaac, and they dwelt there, but their flocks and herds they fed daily in Shechem, for there was there in those days good and fat pasture, and Jacob and his sons and all their household dwelt in the valley of Hebron.

(Jasher 41:2)
And it was in those days, in that year, being the hundred and sixth year of the life of Jacob, in the tenth year of Jacob's coming from Padan-aram, that Leah the wife of Jacob died; she was fifty-one years old when she died in Hebron.

(Jasher 41:3)
And Jacob and his sons buried her in the cave of the field of Machpelah, which is in Hebron, which Abraham had bought from the children of Heth, for the possession of a burial place.

(Jasher 41:4)
And the sons of Jacob dwelt with their father in the valley of Hebron, and all the inhabitants of the land knew their strength and their fame went throughout the land.

~ ~ ~

(Jubilees 36:1)
And in the sixth year of this week, Isaac called his two sons Esau and Jacob, and they came to him, and he said to them: My sons, I am going the way of my fathers, to the eternal house where my fathers are.

(Jubilees 36:2)
Wherefore bury me near Abraham my father, in the double cave in the field of Ephron the Hittite, where Abraham purchased a sepulcher to bury in; in the sepulcher which I dug for myself, there bury me.

(Jubilees 36:3)
And this I command you, my sons, that you practice righteousness and uprightness on the earth, so that the Lord may bring on you all that the Lord said that he would do to Abraham and to his seed.

(Jubilees 36:4)
And love one another, my sons, your brothers as a man who loves his own soul, and let each seek in what he may benefit his brother, and act together on the earth; and let them love each other as their own souls.

(Jubilees 36:5)
And concerning the question of idols, I command and admonish you to reject them and hate them, and love them not, for they are full of deception for those that worship them and for those that bow down to them.

(Jubilees 36:6)
Remember you, my sons, the Lord God of Abraham your father, and how I too worshipped Him and served Him in righteousness and in joy, that He might multiply you and

increase your seed as the stars of heaven in multitude, and establish you on the earth as the plant of righteousness which will not be rooted out to all the generations forever.

(Jubilees 36:7)
And now I shall make you swear a great oath - for there is no oath which is greater than it by the name glorious and honored and great and splendid and wonderful and mighty, which created the heavens and the earth and all things together - that you will fear Him and worship Him.

(Jubilees 36:8)
And that each will love his brother with affection and righteousness, and that neither will desire evil against his brother from here after, forever all the days of your life so that you may prosper in all your deeds and not be destroyed.

(Jubilees 36:9)
And if either of you devises evil against his brother, know that from here after, everyone that devises evil against his brother shall fall into his hand, and shall be rooted out of the land of the living, and his seed shall be destroyed from under heaven.

(Jubilees 36:10)
But on the day of turbulence and execration and indignation and anger, with flaming devouring fire as He burnt Sodom, so likewise will He burn his land and his city and all that is his, and he shall be blotted out of the book of the discipline of the children of men, and not be recorded in the book of life, but in that which is appointed to destruction, and he shall depart into eternal execration; so that their condemnation may be always renewed in hate and in execration and in wrath and in torment and in indignation and in plagues and in disease forever.

(Jubilees 36:11)
I say and testify to you, my sons, according to the judgment which shall come on the man who wishes to injure his brother.

(Jubilees 36:12)
And he divided all his possessions between the two on that day and he gave the larger portion to him that was the first-born, and the tower and all that was about it, and all that Abraham possessed at the Well of the Oath.

(Jubilees 36:13)
And he said: This larger portion I will give to the firstborn.

(Jubilees 36:14)
And Esau said, I have sold to Jacob and given my birthright to Jacob; to him let it be given, and I have not a single word to say regarding it, for it is his.

(Jubilees 36:15)
And Isaac said, May a blessing rest on you, my sons, and on your seed this day, for you have given me rest, and my heart is not pained concerning the birthright, lest you shouldest work wickedness on account of it.

(Jubilees 36:16)
May the Most High God bless the man that works righteousness, him and his seed forever.

(Jubilees 36:17)
And he ended commanding them and blessing them, and they eat and drank together before him, and he rejoiced because there was one mind between them, and they went forth from him and rested that day and slept.

(Genesis 35:28) (Jubilees 36:18)
And Isaac slept on his bed that day rejoicing; and he slept the eternal sleep, and died. And the days of Isaac were a hundred and eighty years old. He completed twenty-five weeks and five years; and his two sons Esau and Jacob buried him.

(Genesis 35:29)
And Isaac gave up the ghost, and died, and was gathered to his people, being old and full of days: and his sons Esau and Jacob buried him.

(Jubilees 36:20)
And Jacob dwelt in the mountains of Hebron, in the tower of the land of the sojournings of his father Abraham, and he worshipped the Lord with all his heart and according to the visible commands according as He had divided the days of his generations.

(Jubilees 36:21)
And Leah his wife died in the fourth year of the second week of the forty-fifth jubilee, and he buried her in the double cave near Rebecca his mother to the left of the grave of Sarah, his father's mother.

(Jubilees 36:22)
And all her sons and his sons came to mourn over Leah his wife with him and to comfort him regarding her, for he was lamenting her for he loved her exceedingly after Rachel her sister died;

(Jubilees 36:23)
For she was perfect and upright in all her ways and honored Jacob, and all the days that she lived with him he did not hear from her mouth a harsh word, for she was gentle and

peaceable and upright and honorable.

(Jubilees 36:24)
And he remembered all her deeds which she had done during her life and he lamented her exceedingly; for he loved her with all his heart and with all his soul.

Genesis: Chapter Thirty-Six

(Genesis 36:1)

Now these are the generations of Esau, who is Edom.

(Genesis 36:2)

Esau took his wives of the daughters of Canaan; Adah the daughter of Elon the Hittite, and Aholibamah the daughter of Anah the daughter of Zibeon the Hivite;

(Genesis 36:3)

And Bashemath Ishmael's daughter, sister of Nebajoth.

(Genesis 36:4)

And Adah bore to Esau Eliphaz; and Bashemath bore Reuel;

(Genesis 36:5)

And Aholibamah bore Jeush, and Jaalam, and Korah: these are the sons of Esau, which were born to him in the land of Canaan.

(Genesis 36:6) (Jasher 36:20...) (Jubilees 36:19)

And Esau took his wives, and his sons, and his daughters, and all the persons of his house, and his cattle, and all his beasts, and all his substance, which he had got in the land of Canaan; and went into the country to the land of Edom, to the mountains of Seir and dwelt there from the face of his brother Jacob.

(Genesis 36:7)

For their riches were more than that they might dwell together;

and the land wherein they were strangers could not bear them because of their cattle.

(Genesis 36:8) (...Jasher 36:20, ...38)
Thus, Esau and his children dwelt in the land of Seir the Horite, the inhabitant of the land, in mount Seir and had possessions in the land of Seir, and the children of Esau were fruitful and multiplied exceedingly in the land of Seir: Esau is Edom.

(Genesis 36:9) (Jasher 36:21)
And these are the generations of Esau the father of the Edomites in Mount Seir: that were born to him in the land of Canaan, and the sons of Esau were five.

(Genesis 36:10...) (Jasher 36:22...)
These are the names of Esau's sons; Eliphaz his first born the son of Adah the wife of Esau,

(...Genesis 36:10)
Reuel the son of Bashemath the wife of Esau.

(...Jasher 36:22...)
And Adah... also bare to him Reuel,

(Genesis 36:11) (...Jasher 36:23...)
These are the children of Esau who were born to him in the land of Canaan; And the sons of Eliphaz the son of Esau were Teman, Omar, Zepho, and Gatam, and Kenaz and Amalex.

(Genesis 36:12) (Jasher 36:27...)
And Timna, was concubine to Eliphaz Esau's son; and she bore to Eliphaz Amalek: these were the sons of Adah Esau's wife.

(Genesis 36:13) (...Jasher 36:23)
And these are the sons of Reuel; Nahath, and Zerah, Shammah, and Mizzah: these were the sons of Bashemath Esau's wife.

(Genesis 36:14) (...Jasher 36:22)
And these were the sons of Aholibamah, the daughter of Anah the daughter of Zibeon, Esau's wife: and she bore to Esau Jeush, and Jaalam, and Korah.

(Jasher 36:24)
And the sons of Jeush were Timnah, Alvah, Jetheth; and the sons of Yaalam were Alah, Phinor and Kenaz.

(Jasher 36:25...)
And the sons of Korah were Teman, Mibzar, Magdiel and Eram;

(Genesis 36:15)
These were dukes of the sons of Esau: the sons of Eliphaz the firstborn son of Esau; duke Teman, duke Omar, duke Zepho, duke Kenaz,

(Genesis 36:16)
Duke Korah, duke Gatam, and duke Amalek: these are the dukes that came of Eliphaz in the land of Edom; these were the sons of Adah.

(Genesis 36:17)
And these are the sons of Reuel Esau's son; duke Nahath, duke Zerah, duke Shammah, duke Mizzah: these are the dukes that came of Reuel in the land of Edom; these are the sons of Bashemath Esau's wife.

(Genesis 36:18)

And these are the sons of Aholibamah Esau's wife; duke Jeush, duke Jaalam, duke Korah: these were the dukes that came of Aholibamah the daughter of Anah, Esau's wife.

(Genesis 36:19) (...Jasher 36:25)

These are the families of the sons of Esau, who is Edom, and these are their dukes according to their dukedoms in the land of Seir.

(Genesis 36:20) (Jasher 36:26...)

These are the names of the sons of Seir the Horite, who inhabited the land of Seir; Lotan, and Shobal, and Zibeon, and Anah,

(Genesis 36:21) (...Jasher 36:26)

And Dishon, and Ezer, and Dishan, being seven sons: these are the dukes of the Horites, the children of Seir in the land of Edom.

(Genesis 36:22) (...Jasher 36:27)

And the children of Lotan were Hori and Hemam; and Lotan's sister was Timna, that is Timna who came to Jacob and his sons, and they would not give ear to her, and she went and became a concubine to Eliphaz the son of Esau.

(Genesis 36:23) (Jasher 36:28...)

And the children of Shobal were these; Alvan, and Manahath, and Ebal, Shepho, and Onam.

(Genesis 36:24) (...Jasher 36:28)

And these are the children of Zibeon; both Ajah, and Anah: this was that Anah that found the mules (Yemim) in the wilderness, as he fed the donkeys of Zibeon his father.

(Jasher 36:29)
And while he was feeding his father's donkeys he led them to the wilderness at different times to feed them.

(Jasher 36:30)
And there was a day that he brought them to one of the deserts on the sea shore, opposite the wilderness of the people, and while he was feeding them, behold a very heavy storm came from the other side of the sea and rested upon the donkeys that were feeding there, and they all stood still.

(Jasher 36:31)
And afterward about one hundred and twenty great and terrible animals came out from the wilderness at the other side of the sea, and they all came to the place where the donkeys were, and they placed themselves there.

(Jasher 36:32)
And those animals, from their middle downward, were in the shape of the children of men, and from their middle upward, some had the likeness of bears, and some the likeness of the keephas, with tails behind them from between their shoulders reaching down to the earth, like the tails of the ducheephath, and these animals came and mounted and rode upon these donkeys, and led them away, and they went away to this day.

(Jasher 36:33)
And one of these animals approached Anah and smote him with his tail, and then fled from that place.

(Jasher 36:34)
And when he saw this work he was exceedingly afraid of his life, and he fled and escaped to the city.

(Jasher 36:35)
And he related to his sons and brothers all that had happened to him, and many men went to seek the donkeys but could not find them, and Anah and his brothers went no more to that place from that day following, for they were greatly afraid of their lives.

(Genesis 36:25) (Jasher 36:36...)
And the children of Anah the son of Seir, were these; Dishon, and his sister Aholibamah the daughter of Anah.

(Genesis 36:26) (...Jasher 36:36...)
And these are the children of Dishon; Hemdan, and Eshban, and Ithran, and Cheran.

(Genesis 36:27) (...Jasher 36:36...)
The children of Ezer are these; Bilhan, and Zaavan, and Akan.

(Genesis 36:28) (...Jasher 36:36)
The children of Dishan are these; Uz, and Aran.

(Jasher 36:37...)
These are the families of the children of Seir the Horite.

(Genesis 36:29)
These are the dukes that came of the Horites; duke Lotan, duke Shobal, duke Zibeon, duke Anah,

(Genesis 36:30) (...Jasher 36:37)
Duke Dishon, duke Ezer, duke Dishan: these are the dukes that came of Hori according to their dukedoms, among their dukes in the land of Seir.

(Jubilees 37:1)
And on the day that Isaac the father of Jacob and Esau died, the sons of Esau heard that Isaac had given the portion of the elder to his younger son Jacob and they were very angry.

(Jubilees 37:2)
And they strove with their father, saying Why has your father given Jacob the portion of the elder and passed over you, although you are the elder and Jacob the younger?

(Jubilees 37:3)
And he said to them Because I sold my birthright to Jacob for a small mess of lentils, and on the day my father sent me to hunt and catch and bring him something that he should eat and bless me, he came with guile and brought my father food and drink, and my father blessed him and put me under his hand.

(Jubilees 37:4)
And now our father has caused us to swear, me and him, that we shall not mutually devise evil, either against his brother, and that we shall continue in love and in peace each with his brother and not make our ways corrupt.

(Jubilees 37:5)
And they said to him, We shall not hearken to you to make peace with him; for our strength is greater than his strength, and we are more powerful than he; we shall go against him and slay him, and destroy him and his sons. And if you will not go with us, we shall do hurt to you also.

(Jubilees 37:6)
And now hearken to us: Let us send to Aram and Philistia and Moab and Ammon, and let us choose for ourselves chosen

men who are ardent for battle, and let us go against him and do battle with him, and let us exterminate him from the earth before he grows strong.

(Jubilees 37:7)
And their father said to them, Do not go and do not make war with him lest you fall before him.

(Jubilees 37:8)
And they said to him, This too, is exactly your mode of action from your youth until this day, and you are putting your neck under his yoke.

(Jubilees 37:9)
We shall not hearken to these words. And they sent to Aram, and to Aduram to the friend of their father, and they hired along with them one thousand fighting men, chosen men of war.

(Jubilees 37:10)
And there came to them from Moab and from the children of Ammon, those who were hired, one thousand chosen men, and from Philistia, one thousand chosen men of war, and from Edom and from the Horites one thousand chosen fighting men, and from the Kittim mighty men of war.

(Jubilees 37:11)
And they said to their father: Go forth with them and lead them, else we shall slay you.

(Jubilees 37:12)
And he was filled with wrath and indignation on seeing that his sons were forcing him to go before them to lead them

against Jacob his brother.

(Jubilees 37:13)
But afterward he remembered all the evil which lay hidden in his heart against Jacob his brother; and he remembered not the oath which he had sworn to his father and to his mother that he would devise no evil all his days against Jacob his brother.

(Jubilees 37:14)
And notwithstanding all this, Jacob knew not that they were coming against him to battle, and he was mourning for Leah, his wife, until they approached very near to the tower with four thousand warriors and chosen men of war.

(Jubilees 37:15)
And the men of Hebron sent to him saying, Behold your brother has come against you, to fight you, with four thousand girt with the sword, and they carry shields and weapons; for they loved Jacob more than Esau. So they told him; for Jacob was a more liberal and merciful man than Esau.

(Jubilees 37:16)
But Jacob would not believe until they came very near to the tower.

(Jubilees 37:17)
And he closed the gates of the tower; and he stood on the battlements and spoke to his brother Esau and said, Noble is the comfort wherewith you have come to comfort me for my wife who has died. Is this the oath that you swore to your father and again to your mother before they died? You have broken the oath, and on the moment that you swear to your father you were condemned.

(Jubilees 37:18)
And then Esau answered and said to him, Neither the children of men nor the beasts of the earth have any oath of righteousness which in swearing they have sworn forever; but every day they devise evil one against another, and how each may slay his adversary and foe.

(Jubilees 37:19)
And you do hate me and my children forever. And there is no observing the tie of brotherhood with you.

(Jubilees 37:20)
Hear these words which I declare to you, If the boar can change its skin and make its bristles as soft as wool, Or if it can cause horns to sprout forth on its head like the horns of a stag or of a sheep, Then will I observe the tie of brotherhood with you, And if the breasts separated themselves from their mother, for you have not been a brother to me.

(Jubilees 37:21)
And if the wolves make peace with the lambs so as not to devour or do them violence, And if their hearts are towards them for good, Then there shall be peace in my heart towards you

(Jubilees 37:22)
And if the lion becomes the friend of the ox and makes peace with him, And if he is bound under one yoke with him and ploughs with him, Then will I make peace with you.

(Jubilees 37:23)
And when the raven becomes white as the raza, then know that I have loved you, And shall make peace with you You

shall be rooted out, And your sons shall be rooted out, And there shall be no peace for you.

(Jubilees 37:24)
And when Jacob saw that he was evilly disposed towards him with his heart, and with all his soul as to slay him, and that he had come springing like the wild boar which comes on the spear that pierces and kills it, and recoils not from it;

(Jubilees 37:25)
Then he spoke to his own and to his servants that they should attack him and all his companions.

~ ~ ~

(Jubilees 38:1)
And after that Judah spoke to Jacob, his father, and said to him: Bend your bow, father, and send forth your arrows and cast down the adversary and slay the enemy; and may you have the power, for we shall not slay your brother, for he is such as you, and he is like you let us give him honor.

(Jubilees 38:2)
Then Jacob bent his bow and sent forth the arrow and struck Esau, his brother on his right breast, and slew him.

(Jubilees 38:3)
And again, he sent forth an arrow and struck Adoran the Aramaean, on the left breast, and drove him backward and slew him.

(Jubilees 38:4)
And then went forth the sons of Jacob, they and their servants, dividing themselves into companies on the four sides of the tower.

(Jubilees 38:5)
And Judah went forth in front, and Naphtali and Gad with him and fifty servants with him on the south side of the tower, and they slew all they found before them, and not one individual of them escaped.

(Jubilees 38:6)
And Levi and Dan and Asher went forth on the east side of the tower, and fifty men with them, and they slew the fighting men of Moab and Ammon.

(Jubilees 38:7)
And Reuben and Issachar and Zebulon went forth on the north side of the tower, and fifty men with them, and they slew the fighting men of the Philistines.

(Jubilees 38:8)
And Simeon and Benjamin and Enoch, Reuben's son, went forth on the west side of the tower, and fifty men with them, and they slew of Edom and of the Horites four hundred men, stout warriors; and six hundred fled, and four of the sons of Esau fled with them, and left their father lying slain, as he had fallen on the hill which is in Aduram.

(Jubilees 38:9)
And the sons of Jacob pursued after them to the mountains of Seir. And Jacob buried his brother on the hill which is in Aduram, and he returned to his house.

(Jubilees 38:10)
And the sons of Jacob pressed hard on the sons of Esau in the mountains of Seir, and bowed their necks so that they became servants of the sons of Jacob.

(Jubilees 38:11)
And they sent to their father to inquire whether they should make peace with them or slay them.

(Jubilees 38:12)
And Jacob sent word to his sons that they should make peace, and they made peace with them, and placed the yoke of servitude on them, so that they paid tribute to Jacob and to his sons always.

(Jubilees 38:13)
And they continued to pay tribute to Jacob until the day that he went down into Egypt.

(Jubilees 38:14)
And the sons of Edom have not got quit of the yoke of servitude which the twelve sons of Jacob had imposed on them until this day.

(Genesis 36:31) (Jubilees 38:15)
And these are the kings that reigned in the land of Edom, before there reigned any king over the children of Israel until this day in the land of Edom.

(Genesis 36:32) (Jubilees 38:16)
And Bela the son of Beor reigned in Edom: and the name of his city was Dinhabah.

(Genesis 36:33) (Jubilees 38:17)
And Bela died, and Jobab the son of Zerah of Bozrah reigned in his stead.

(Genesis 36:34) (Jubilees 38:18)
And Jobab died, and Husham of the land of Temani reigned in his stead.

(Genesis 36:35) (Jubilees 38:19)
And Husham died, and Hadad the son of Bedad who smote Midian in the field of Moab, reigned in his stead: and the name of his city was Avith.

(Genesis 36:36) (Jubilees 38:20)
And Hadad, and Samlah of Masrekah reigned in his stead.

(Genesis 36:37) (Jubilees 38:21)
And Samlah died, and Saul of Rehoboth by the river reigned in his stead.

(Genesis 36:38) (Jubilees 38:22)
And Saul died, and Baalhanan the son of Achbor reigned in his stead.

(Genesis 36:39) (Jubilees 38:23)
And Baalhanan the son of Achbor died, and Hadar reigned in his stead: and the name of his city was Pau; and his wife's name was Mehetabel, the daughter of Matred, the daughter of Mezahab.

(Jubilees 38:24)
These are the kings who reigned in the land of Edom.

(Genesis 36:40)

And these are the names of the dukes that came of Esau, according to their families, after their places, by their names; duke Timnah, duke Alvah, duke Jetheth,

(Genesis 36:41)

Duke Aholibamah, duke Elah, duke Pinon,

(Genesis 36:42)

Duke Kenaz, duke Teman, duke Mibzar,

(Genesis 36:43)

Duke Magdiel, duke Iram: these be the dukes of Edom, according to their habitations in the land of their possession: he is Esau the father of the Edomites.

Genesis: Chapter Thirty-Seven

(Genesis 37:1)

And Jacob dwelt in the land wherein his father was a stranger, in the land of Canaan.

(Jasher 41:5)

And Joseph the son of Jacob, and his brother Benjamin, the sons of Rachel, the wife of Jacob, were yet young in those days, and did not go out with their brothers during their battles in all the cities of the Amorites.

(Jasher 41:6...)

And when Joseph saw the strength of his brothers, and their greatness, he praised them and extolled them, but he ranked himself greater than them, and extolled himself above them;

(Genesis 37:2) (Jasher 41:7)

These are the generations of Jacob. Joseph, being seventeen years old, was feeding the flock with his brothers; And when Joseph saw that his father loved him more than his brothers, he continued to exalt himself above his brothers. And the lad was with the sons of Bilhah, and with the sons of Zilpah, his father's wives: and Joseph brought to his father their evil reports concerning them.

(Genesis 37:3) (...Jasher 41:6)

Now Israel, his father, loved Joseph more than all his children, because he was the son of his old age: and through his love toward him, he made him a coat of many colors.

(Genesis 37:4) (Jasher 41:8)

And when his brothers, the sons of Jacob, saw the whole of Joseph's conduct toward them, and that their father loved him more than all his brothers, they hated him, and could not speak peaceably to him all the days.

(Jasher 41:9)

And Joseph was seventeen years old, and he was still magnifying himself above his brothers, and thought of raising himself above them.

(Genesis 37:5) (Jasher 41:10...)

And at that time, Joseph dreamed a dream, and he came to his brothers and he told his brothers his dream: and they hated him yet the more.

(Genesis 37:6) (...Jasher 41:10...)

And he said to them, Hear, I pray, this dream which I have dreamed:

(Genesis 37:7) (...Jasher 41:10)

For, behold, we were all binding sheaves in the field, and, lo, my sheaf arose and placed itself upon the ground, and also stood upright; and, behold, your sheaves stood round about, and made obeisance to my sheaf.

(Genesis 37:8) (Jasher 41:11)

And his brothers answered him and said to him, What does this dream mean that you dreamed? Shall you indeed imagine in your heart to reign over us? Or shall you indeed have dominion over us? And they hated him yet the more for his dreams, and for his words.

(Jasher 41:12)
And he still came, and told the thing to his father Jacob, and Jacob kissed Joseph when he heard these words from his mouth, and Jacob blessed Joseph.

(Jasher 41:13)
And when the sons of Jacob saw that their father had blessed Joseph and had kissed him, and that he loved him exceedingly, they became jealous of him and hated him the more.

(Genesis 37:9) (Jasher 41:14...)
And after this Joseph dreamed yet another dream, and told it to his brothers, and Joseph said, to his father and brothers, Behold, I have dreamed a dream more; and, behold, the sun and the moon and the eleven stars made obeisance to me.

(Genesis 37:10) (...Jasher 41:14, 15, 16)
And he told it to his father, and to his brothers: and his father heard the words of Joseph and his dream, and seeing that his brothers hated Joseph on account of this matter, Jacob rebuked him before his brothers on account of this thing, and said to him, What is the meaning of this dream that you have dreamed, and this magnifying yourself before your brothers who are older than you are? Shall I and your mother and your brothers indeed come to bow down ourselves to you to the earth? Do you imagine this in your heart that you speak these things?

(Genesis 37:11) (Jasher 41:17)
And his brothers envied him on account of his words and dreams, and they continued to hate him; but Jacob his father observed the saying and reserved the dreams in his heart.

(Genesis 37:12) (Jasher 41:18)

And his brothers, the sons of Jacob, went to feed their father's flock in Shechem, for they were still herdsmen in those days; and while the sons of Jacob were that day feeding in Shechem they delayed, and the time of gathering in the cattle was passed, and they had not arrived.

(Jasher 41:19)

And Jacob saw that his sons were delayed in Shechem, and Jacob said within himself, Peradventure the people of Shechem have risen up to fight against them, therefore they have delayed coming this day.

(Genesis 37:13) (Jasher 41:20...) (Jubilees 34:10...)

And in the seventh year of this week, Israel called Joseph his son and said to Joseph, Don't your brothers feed the flock in Shechem this day? And behold they have not yet come back; come, and I will send you to them. And he said to him, Here am I.

(Genesis 37:14) (...Jasher 41:20, 21) (...Jubilees 34:10...)

And he said to him, Go now therefore, I pray, and see where they are, whether it be well with your brothers, and well with the flocks; and bring me word again. So he sent him from his house out of the vale of Hebron, and Joseph came for his brothers to the land of Shechem and could not find them, and Joseph went about the field which was near Shechem, to see where his brothers had turned, and he missed his road in the wilderness, and knew not which way he should go.

(Genesis 37:15) (Jasher 41:22...)

And a certain man, an angel of the Lord, found him, and, behold, he was wandering in the road toward the field: and the man asked him, saying, What are you seeking?

(Genesis 37:16) (...Jasher 41:22...)

And Joseph said to the angel of the Lord, I seek my brothers: tell me, I pray, where they feed their flocks.

(Genesis 37:17) (...Jasher 41:22, 23) (...Jubilees 34:10)

And the man, the angel of the Lord, said to Joseph, I saw your brothers feeding here, but they have departed from here; for I heard them say, Let us go to Dothan. And Joseph hearkened to the voice of the angel of the Lord, and he went after his brothers in Dothan, and found them in the land of Dothan feeding the flock.

(Genesis 37:18) (Jasher 41:24) (Jubilees 34:11...)

And Joseph advanced to his brothers, and when they saw him afar off, even before he came near to them, they dealt treacherously with him, and they conspired against him to slay him.

(Genesis 37:19) (Jasher 41:25...)

And they said one to another, Behold, this dreamer comes to us this day.

(Genesis 37:20) (...Jasher 41:25)

Come now therefore, and let us slay him, and cast him into some pit that is in the wilderness, and when his father shall seek him from us, we will say, Some evil beast has devoured him: and we shall see what will become of his dreams.

(Genesis 37:21) (Jasher 41:26...)

And Reuben heard the words of his brothers concerning Joseph, and he delivered him out of their hands; and said, Let us not kill him.

(Genesis 37:22) (...Jasher 41:26)

And Reuben said to them, Do not shed blood. You should not do this thing, for how can we look up to our father Jacob? But cast him into this pit that is in the wilderness, and lay no hand on him; that he might rid him out of their hands, to deliver him to his father again.

(Genesis 37:23) (Jasher 41:27)

And it came to pass, when Joseph was come to his brothers, that he sat before them, and they rose upon him and seized him and smote him to the earth, and they stripped Joseph out of his coat, his coat of many colors that was on him;

(Genesis 37:24) (Jasher 41:28)

And they took him, and cast him into a pit: and the pit was empty, there was no water in it; but serpents and scorpions. And Joseph was afraid of the serpents and scorpions that were in the pit. And Joseph cried out with a loud voice, and the Lord hid the serpents and scorpions in the sides of the pit, and they did no harm to Joseph.

(Jasher 41:29)

And Joseph called out from the pit to his brothers, and said to them, What have I done to you, and in what have I sinned? Why do you not fear the Lord concerning me? Am I not of your bones and flesh, and is not Jacob your father, my father? Why do you do this thing to me this day, and how will you be able to look up to our father Jacob?

(Jasher 41:30)

And he continued to cry out and call to his brothers from the pit, and he said, O Judah, Simeon, and Levi, my brothers, lift me up from the place of darkness in which you have placed me, and come this day to have compassion on me, ye children of the Lord, and sons of Jacob my father. And if I have sinned to you, are you not the sons of Abraham, Isaac, and Jacob? If they saw an orphan they had compassion over him, or one that was hungry, they gave him bread to eat, or one that was thirsty, they gave him water to drink, or one that was naked, they covered him with garments!

(Jasher 41:31)
And how then will you withhold your pity from your brother, for I am of your flesh and bones, and if I have sinned to you, surely you will do this on account of my father!

(Jasher 41:32)
And Joseph spoke these words from the pit, and his brothers could not listen to him, nor incline their ears to the words of Joseph, and Joseph was crying and weeping in the pit.

(Jasher 41:33)
And Joseph said, O that my father knew, this day, the act which my brothers have done to me, and the words which they have this day spoken to me.

(Jasher 41:34)
And all his brothers heard his cries and weeping in the pit, and his brothers went and removed themselves from the pit, so that they might not hear the cries of Joseph and his weeping in the pit.

(Genesis 37:25...) (Jasher 42:1)
And they went and went and sat on the opposite side, about the distance of a bow-shot, and they sat down to eat bread: and while they were eating, they held counsel together what was to be done with him, whether to slay him or to bring him back to his father.

(...Genesis 37:25) (Jasher 42:2)

They were holding the counsel, and when they lifted up their eyes and looked, and, behold, there was a company of Ishmaelites came from a distance by the road of Gilead with their camels bearing spices and balm and myrrh, going to carry it down to Egypt.

(Genesis 37:26) (Jasher 42:3)

And Judah said to his brothers, What profit is it if we slay our brother, and conceal his blood? Peradventure God will require him from us; this then is the counsel proposed concerning him, which you shall do to him: Behold this company of Ishmaelites going down to Egypt;

(Genesis 37:27) (Jasher 42:4) (...Jubilees 34:11...)

Now therefore, come, and let us sell him to the Ishmaelites, and let not our hand be on him; let us dispose of him to them, and they will lead him along with them, and he will be lost among the people of the land, and we will not put him to death with our own hands; for he is our brother and our flesh. And the proposal pleased his brothers and they changed their minds and were content and they did according to the word of Judah.

(Genesis 37:28...) (Jasher 42:5)

And while they were discoursing about this matter, and before the company of Ishmaelites had come up to them. Then there passed by them seven Midianites merchantmen, and as they passed they were thirsty, and they lifted up their eyes and saw the pit in which Joseph was immured, and they looked, and behold every species of bird was upon him;

(Jasher 42:6)

And these Midianites ran to the pit to drink water, for they thought that it contained water, and on coming before the pit they heard the voice of Joseph crying and weeping in the pit, and they looked down into the pit, and they saw and behold there was a youth of comely appearance and well favored.

(...Genesis 37:28...) (Jasher 42:7)
And they called to him and said, Who are you and who brought you hither, and who placed you in this pit, in the wilderness? And they all assisted to raise up Joseph and they drew and lifted up Joseph out of the pit, and took him and went away on their journey and passed by his brothers.

(Jasher 42:8)
And the brothers said to the Midianites, Why do you do this, to take our servant from us and to go away? Surely we placed this youth in the pit because he rebelled against us, and you come and bring him up and lead him away; now then give us back our servant.

(Jasher 42:9)
And the Midianites answered and said to the sons of Jacob, Is this your servant, or does this man attend you? Peradventure you are all his servants, for he is more comely and well favored than any of you, and why do you all speak falsely to us?

(Jasher 42:10)
Now therefore we will not listen to your words, nor attend to you, for we found the youth in the pit in the wilderness, and we took him; we will therefore go on.

(Jasher 42:11)
And all the sons of Jacob approached them and rose up to them and said to them, Give us back our servant, and why will you all die by the edge of the sword? And the Midianites cried out against them, and they drew their swords, and approached

to fight with the sons of Jacob.

(Jasher 42:12)
And behold Simeon rose up from his seat against them, and sprang upon the ground and drew his sword and approached the Midianites and he gave a terrible shout before them, so that his shouting was heard at a distance, and the earth shook at Simeon's shouting.

(Jasher 42:13)
And the Midianites were terrified on account of Simeon and the noise of his shouting, and they fell upon their faces, and were excessively alarmed.

(Jasher 42:14)
And Simeon said to them, Verily I am Simeon, the son of Jacob the Hebrew, who have, only with my brother, destroyed the city of Shechem and the cities of the Amorites; so shall God moreover do to me, that if all your brothers the people of Midian, and also the kings of Canaan, were to come with you, they could not fight against me.

(Jasher 42:15)
Now therefore give us back the youth whom you have taken, lest I give your flesh to the birds of the skies and the beasts of the earth.

(Jasher 42:16)
And the Midianites were more afraid of Simeon, and they approached the sons of Jacob with terror and fright, and with pathetic words, saying,

(Jasher 42:17)
Surely you have said that the young man is your servant, and

that he rebelled against you, and therefore you placed him in the pit; what then will you do with a servant who rebels against his master? Now therefore sell him to us, and we will give you all that you require for him; and the Lord was pleased to do this in order that the sons of Jacob should not slay their brother.

(Jasher 42:18)
And the Midianites saw that Joseph was of a comely appearance and well-favored; they desired him in their hearts and were urgent to purchase him from his brothers.

(Jasher 42:19)
And the sons of Jacob hearkened to the Midianites and they sold their brother Joseph to them for twenty pieces of silver, and Reuben their brother was not with them, and the Midianites took Joseph and continued their journey to Gilead.

(Jasher 42:20)
They were going along the road, and the Midianites repented of what they had done, in having purchased the young man, and one said to the other, What is this thing that we have done, in taking this youth from the Hebrews, who is of comely appearance and well favored.

(Jasher 42:21)
Perhaps this youth is stolen from the land of the Hebrews, and why then have we done this thing? And if he should be sought for and found in our hands we shall die through him.

(Jasher 42:22)
Now surely hardy and powerful men have sold him to us, the strength of one of whom you saw this day; perhaps they stole him from his land with their might and with their powerful

arm, and have therefore sold him to us for the small value which we gave to them.

(Jasher 42:23)
And while they were thus discoursing together, they looked, and behold the company of Ishmaelites which was coming at first, and which the sons of Jacob saw, was advancing toward the Midianites, and the Midianites said to each other, Come let us sell this youth to the company of Ishmaelites who are coming toward us, and we will take for him the little that we gave for him, and we will be delivered from his evil.

(...Genesis 37:28...) (Jasher 42:24) (...Jubilees 34:11...)
And they did so, and they reached the Ishmaelites, and the Midianites sold Joseph to the Ishmaelites merchants for twenty pieces of silver which they had given for him to his brothers.

(Jasher 42:25)
And the Midianites went on their road to Gilead, and the Ishmaelites took Joseph and they let him ride upon one of the camels, and they were leading him to Egypt.

(Jasher 42:26)
And Joseph heard that the Ishmaelites were proceeding to Egypt, and Joseph lamented and wept at this thing that he was to be so far removed from the land of Canaan, from his father, and he wept bitterly while he was riding upon the camel, and one of their men observed him, and made him go down from the camel and walk on foot, and notwithstanding this Joseph continued to cry and weep, and he said, O my father, my father.

(Jasher 42:27)
And one of the Ishmaelites rose up and smote Joseph upon the cheek, and still he continued to weep; and Joseph was fatigued in the road, and was unable to proceed on account of the bitterness of his soul, and they all smote him and afflicted him in the road, and they terrified him in order that he might cease from weeping.

(Jasher 42:28)
And the Lord saw the ambition of Joseph and his trouble, and the Lord brought down upon those men darkness and confusion, and the hand of every one that smote him became withered.

(Jasher 42:29)
And they said to each other, What is this thing that God has done to us in the road? And they knew not that this befell them on account of Joseph. And the men proceeded on the road, and they passed along the road of Ephrath where Rachel was buried.

(Jasher 42:30)
And Joseph reached his mother's grave, and Joseph hastened and ran to his mother's grave, and fell upon the grave and wept.

(Jasher 42:31)
And Joseph cried aloud upon his mother's grave, and he said, O my mother, my mother, O you who gave me birth, awake now, and rise and see your son, how he has been sold for a slave, and no one to pity him.

(Jasher 42:32)
O rise and see your son, weep with me on account of my

troubles, and see the heart of my brothers.

(Jasher 42:33)
Arouse my mother, arouse, awake from your sleep for me, and direct your battles against my brothers. O how have they stripped me of my coat, and sold me already twice for a slave, and separated me from my father, and there is no one to pity me.

(Jasher 42:34)
Arouse and lay your cause against them before God, and see whom God will justify in the judgment, and whom he will condemn.

(Jasher 42:35)
Rise, O my mother, rise, awake from your sleep and see my father how his soul is with me this day, and comfort him and ease his heart.

(Jasher 42:36)
And Joseph continued to speak these words, and Joseph cried aloud and wept bitterly upon his mother's grave; and he ceased speaking, and from bitterness of heart he became still as a stone upon the grave.

(Jasher 42:37)
And Joseph heard a voice speaking to him from beneath the ground, which answered him with bitterness of heart, and with a voice of weeping and praying in these words:

(Jasher 42:38)
My son, my son Joseph, I have heard the voice of your weeping and the voice of your lamentation; I have seen your tears; I know your troubles, my son, and it grieves me for your sake,

and abundant grief is added to my grief.

(Jasher 42:39)
Now therefore my son, Joseph my son, hope to the Lord, and wait for him and do not fear, for the Lord is with you, he will deliver you from all trouble.

(Jasher 42:40)
Rise my son, go down to Egypt with your masters, and do not fear, for the Lord is with you, my son. And she continued to speak like to these words to Joseph, and she was still.

(Jasher 42:41)
And Joseph heard this, and he wondered greatly at this, and he continued to weep; and after this one of the Ishmaelites observed him crying and weeping upon the grave, and his anger was kindled against him, and he drove him from there, and he smote him and cursed him.

(Jasher 42:42)
And Joseph said to the men, May I find grace in your sight to take me back to my father's house, and he will give you abundance of riches.

(Jasher 42:43)
And they answered him, saying, Are you not a slave, and where is your father? And if you had a father you would not already twice have been sold for a slave for so little value; and their anger was still roused against him, and they continued to smite him and to chastise him, and Joseph wept bitterly.

(Jasher 42:44)
And the Lord saw Joseph's affliction, and Lord again smote these men, and chastised them, and the Lord caused darkness

to envelope them upon the earth, and the lightning flashed and the thunder roared, and the earth shook at the voice of the thunder and of the mighty wind, and the men were terrified and knew not where they should go.

(Jasher 42:45)
And the beasts and camels stood still, and they led them, but they would not go, they smote them, and they crouched upon the ground; and the men said to each other, What is this that God has done to us? What are our transgressions, and what are our sins that this thing has thus befallen us?

(Jasher 42:46)
And one of them answered and said to them, Perhaps on account of the sin of afflicting this slave has this thing happened this day to us; now therefore implore him strongly to forgive us, and then we shall know on whose account this evil befalls us, and if God shall have compassion over us, then we shall know that all this comes to us on account of the sin of afflicting this slave.

(Jasher 42:47)
And the men did so, and they supplicated Joseph and pressed him to forgive them; and they said, We have sinned to the Lord and to you, now therefore vouchsafe to request of your God that he shall put away this death from among us, for we have sinned to him.

(Jasher 42:48)
And Joseph did according to their words, and the Lord hearkened to Joseph, and the Lord put away the plague which he had inflicted upon those men on account of Joseph, and the beasts rose up from the ground and they conducted them, and they went on, and the raging storm abated and the earth became tranquilized, and the men proceeded on their journey

to go down to Egypt, and the men knew that this evil had befallen them on account of Joseph.

(Jasher 42:49)
And they said to each other, Behold we know that it was on account of his affliction that this evil befell us; now therefore why shall we bring this death upon our souls? Let us hold counsel what to do to this slave.

(Jasher 42:50)
And one answered and said, Surely he told us to bring him back to his father; now therefore come, let us take him back and we will go to the place that he will tell us, and take from his family the price that we gave for him and we will then go away.

(Jasher 42:51)
And one answered again and said, Behold, this counsel is very good, but we cannot do so for the way is very far from us, and we cannot go out of our road.

(Jasher 42:52)
And one more answered and said to them, This is the counsel to be adopted, we will not swerve from it; behold we are this day going to Egypt, and when we shall have come to Egypt, we will sell him there at a high price, and we will be delivered from his evil.

(Jasher 42:53)
And this thing pleased the men and they did so, and they continued their journey to Egypt with Joseph.

(...Genesis 37:28) (Jasher 44:1...) (...Jubilees 34:11...)
And they brought Joseph into Egypt.

(Jasher 43:1)
And when the sons of Jacob had sold their brother Joseph to the Midianites, their hearts were smitten on account of him, and they repented of their acts, and they sought for him to bring him back, but could not find him.

(Genesis 37:29...) (Jasher 43:2)
And Reuben returned to the pit in which Joseph had been put, in order to lift him out, and restore him to his father, and Reuben stood by the pit, and he heard not a word, and he called out Joseph! Joseph! And no one answered or uttered a word.

(...Genesis 37:29) (Jasher 43:3, 4...)
And Reuben said, Joseph has died through fright, or some serpent has caused his death; and Reuben descended into the pit, and he searched for Joseph and, behold, Joseph was not in the pit; and he came out again. And Reuben rent his clothes and he said, The child is not there, and how shall I reconcile my father about him if he be dead?

(Genesis 37:30) (...Jasher 43:4)
And he returned to his brothers, and found them grieving on account of Joseph, and counseling together how to reconcile their father about him, and Reuben said to his brothers, I came to the pit and behold, the child is not there, what then shall we say to our father, for my father will only seek the lad from me; and I, where shall I go?

(Jasher 43:5)
And his brothers answered him saying, Thus and thus we did, and our hearts afterward smote us on account of this act, and we now sit to seek a pretext how we shall reconcile our father to it.

(Jasher 43:6)
And Reuben said to them, What is this you have done to bring down the gray hairs of our father in sorrow to the grave? The thing is not good, that you have done.

(Jasher 43:7)
And Reuben sat with them, and they all rose up and swore to each other not to tell this thing to Jacob, and they all said, The man who will tell this to our father or his household, or who will report this to any of the children of the land, we will all rise up against him and slay him with the sword.

(Jasher 43:8)
And the sons of Jacob feared each other in this matter, from the youngest to the oldest, and no one spoke a word, and they concealed the thing in their hearts.

(Jasher 43:9)
And they afterward sat down to determine and invent something to say to their father Jacob concerning all these things.

(Jasher 43:10)
And Issachar said to them, Here is an advice for you if it seem good in your eyes to do this thing, take the coat which belongs to Joseph and tear it, and kill a kid of the goats and dip it in its blood.

(Jasher 43:11)
And send it to our father and when he sees it, he will say an evil beast has devoured him, therefore tear ye his coat and behold his blood will be upon his coat, and by your doing this we shall be free of our father's murmurings.

(Jasher 43:12)
And Issachar's advice pleased them, and they hearkened to him and they did according to the word of Issachar which he had counseled them.

(Genesis 37:31) (Jasher 43:13...) (Jubilees 34:12...)
And the sons of Jacob hastened and took Joseph's coat and tore it, and killed a kid of the goats, and dipped the coat in the blood of the kid, and then trampled it in the dust;

(Genesis 37:32) (...Jasher 43:13) (...Jubilees 34:12)
And they sent the coat of many colors, and they brought it to Jacob their father by the hand of Naphtali on the tenth of the seventh month and they commanded him to say these words:

(Genesis 37:32) (Jasher 43:14)
Saying, We had gathered in the cattle and had come as far as the road to Shechem and farther, when we found this coat upon the road in the wilderness dipped in blood and in dust; know now whether it be your son's coat or not.

(Jasher 43:15)
And Naphtali went and he came to his father and he gave him the coat, and he spoke to him all the words which his brothers had commanded him.

(Genesis 37:33...) (Jasher 43:16)
And Jacob saw Joseph's coat and he knew it, and he fell upon his face to the ground, and became as still as a stone, and he afterward rose up and cried out with a loud and weeping voice and he said, It is the coat of my son Joseph!

(Jasher 43:17)
And Jacob hastened and sent one of his servants to his sons,

who went to them and found them coming along the road with the flock.

(Jasher 43:18)
And the sons of Jacob came to their father about evening, and behold their garments were torn and dust was upon their heads, and they found their father crying out and weeping with a loud voice.

(Jasher 43:19)
And Jacob said to his sons, Tell me truly what evil have you this day suddenly brought upon me? And they answered their father Jacob, saying, We were coming along this day after the flock had been gathered in, and we came as far as the city of Shechem by the road in the wilderness, and we found this coat filled with blood upon the ground, and we knew it and we sent to you if you could know it.

(...Genesis 37:33) (Jasher 43:20) (Jubilees 34:13...)
And Jacob heard the words of his sons and he cried out with a loud voice, and he mourned all that night, for they had brought it to him in the evening, and he became feverish with mourning for his death, and he said, It is my son's coat; an evil beast has devoured him; Joseph is without doubt rent in pieces for I sent him this day to see whether it was well with you and well with the flocks and to bring me word again from you, and he went as I commanded him, and this has happened to him this day while I thought my son was with you.

(Jasher 43:21)
And the sons of Jacob answered and said, He did not come to us, neither have we seen him from the time of our going out from you until now.

(Genesis 37:34) (Jasher 43:22)
And when Jacob heard their words he again cried out aloud, and he rose up and rent his clothes, and put sackcloth on his loins, and he wept bitterly and he mourned for his son many days and lifted up his voice in weeping and exclaimed and said these words.

(Jasher 43:23)
Joseph my son, O my son Joseph, I sent you this day after the welfare of your brothers, and behold you have been torn in pieces; through my hand has this happened to my son.

(Jasher 43:24)
It grieves me for you Joseph my son, it grieves me for you; how sweet you were to me during life, and now how exceedingly bitter is your death to me.

(Jasher 43:25)
o that I had died in your stead Joseph my son, for it grieves me sadly for you my son, O my son, my son. Joseph my son, where are you, and where have you been drawn? Arise, arise from your place, and come and see my grief for you, O my son Joseph.

(Jasher 43:26)
Come now and number the tears gushing from my eyes down my cheeks, and bring them up before the Lord, that his anger may turn from me.

(Jasher 43:27)
o Joseph my son, how did you fall, by the hand of one by whom no one had fallen from the beginning of the world to this day; for you have been put to death by the smiting of an enemy, inflicted with cruelty, but surely I know that this has

happened to you, on account of the multitude of my sins.

(Jasher 43:28)
Arouse now and see how bitter is my trouble for you my son, although I did not rear you, nor fashion you, nor give you breath and soul, but it was God who formed you and built your bones and covered them with flesh, and breathed in your nostrils the breath of life, and then he gave you to me.

(Jasher 43:29)
Now truly God who gave you to me, he has taken you from me, and such then has befallen you.

(Jasher 43:30)
And Jacob continued to speak like to these words concerning Joseph, and he wept bitterly; he fell to the ground and became still.

(Jasher 43:31)
And all the sons of Jacob seeing their father's trouble, they repented of what they had done, and they also wept bitterly.

(Jasher 43:32)
And Judah rose up and lifted his father's head from the ground, and placed it upon his lap, and he wiped his father's tears from his cheeks, and Judah wept an exceeding great weeping, while his father's head was reclining upon his lap, still as a stone.

(Jasher 43:33)
And the sons of Jacob saw their father's trouble, and they lifted up their voices and continued to weep, and Jacob was yet lying upon the ground still as a stone.

(Genesis 37:35) (Jasher 43:34) (Jubilees 34:14)
And all his sons and all his daughters and his servants and his servant's children rose up and stood round him to comfort him; but he refused to be comforted for his son; and he said, For I will go down into the grave to my son mourning. Thus, his father wept for him.

(Jasher 43:35) (...Jubilees 34:13)
And the whole household of Jacob rose up and mourned a great mourning with him that day, and they were grieving and mourning with him all that day on account of Joseph and their father's trouble, and the intelligence reached Isaac, the son of Abraham, the father of Jacob, and he wept bitterly on account of Joseph, he and all his household, and he went from the place where he dwelt in Hebron, and his men with him, and he comforted Jacob his son, and he refused to be comforted.

(Jubilees 34:15)
And on that day Bilhah heard that Joseph had perished, and she died mourning him, and she was living in Qafratef, and Dinah also, his daughter, died after Joseph had perished.

(Jubilees 34:16)
And there came these three mournings on Israel in one month. And they buried Bilhah over against the tomb of Rachel, and Dinah also. His daughter, they buried there.

(Jasher 43:36)
And after this, Jacob rose up from the ground, and his tears were running down his cheeks, and he said to his sons, Rise up and take your swords and your bows, and go forth into the field, and seek whether you can find my son's body and bring it to me that I may bury it.

(Jasher 43:37)
Seek also, I pray you, among the beasts and hunt them, and that which shall come the first before you seize and bring it to me, perhaps the Lord will this day pity my affliction, and prepare before you that which tore my son in pieces, and bring it to me, and I will avenge the cause of my son.

(Jasher 43:38)
And his sons did as their father had commanded them, and they rose up early in the morning, and each took his sword and his bow in his hand, and they went forth into the field to hunt the beasts.

(Jasher 43:39)
And Jacob was still crying aloud and weeping and walking to and fro in the house, and smiting his hands together, saying, Joseph my son, Joseph my son.

(Jasher 43:40)
And the sons of Jacob went into the wilderness to seize the beasts, and behold a wolf came toward them, and they seized him, and brought him to their father, and they said to him, This is the first we have found, and we have brought him to you as you commanded us, and your son's body we could not find.

(Jasher 43:41)
And Jacob took the beast from the hands of his sons, and he cried out with a loud and weeping voice, holding the beast in his hand, and he spoke with a bitter heart to the beast, Why did you devour my son Joseph, and how did you have no fear of the God of the earth, or of my trouble for my son Joseph?

(Jasher 43:42)
And you devoured my son for naught, because he committed no violence, and thereby rendered me culpable on his account, therefore God will require him that is persecuted.

(Jasher 43:43)
And the Lord opened the mouth of the beast in order to comfort Jacob with its words, and it answered Jacob and spoke these words to him,

(Jasher 43:44)
As God lives who created us in the earth, and as your soul lives, my lord, I did not see your son, neither did I tear him to pieces, but from a distant land I also came to seek my son who went from me this day, and I know not whether he be living or dead.

(Jasher 43:45)
And I came this day into the field to seek my son, and your sons found me, and seized me and increased my grief, and have this day brought me before you, and I have now spoken all my words to you.

(Jasher 43:46)
And now therefore, O son of man, I am in your hands, and do to me this day as it may seem good in your sight, but by the life of God who created me, I did not see your son, nor did I tear him to pieces, neither has the flesh of man entered my mouth all the days of my life.

(Jasher 43:47)
And when Jacob heard the words of the beast he was greatly astonished, and sent forth the beast from his hand, and she went her way.

(Jasher 43:48)
And Jacob was still crying aloud and weeping for Joseph day after day, and he mourned for his son many days.

~ ~ ~

(Jubilees 34:17)
And he mourned for Joseph one year, and did not cease, for he said Let me go down to the grave mourning for my son.

(Jubilees 34:18)
For this reason, it is ordained for the children of Israel that they should afflict themselves on the tenth of the seventh month -on the day that the news which made him weep for Joseph came to Jacob his father- that they should make atonement for themselves thereon with a young goat on the tenth of the seventh month, once a year, for their sins; for they had grieved the affection of their father regarding Joseph his son.

(Jubilees 34:19)
And this day has been ordained that they should grieve thereon for their sins, and for all their transgressions and for all their errors, so that they might cleanse themselves on that day once a year.

~ ~ ~

(Jasher 44:1)
And the sons of Ishmael who had bought Joseph from the Midianites, who had bought him from his brothers, went to Egypt with Joseph, and they came upon the borders of Egypt, and when they came near to Egypt, they met four men of the sons of Medan the son of Abraham, who had gone forth from the land of Egypt on their journey.

(Jasher 44:2)
And the Ishmaelites said to them, Do you desire to purchase this slave from us? And they said, Deliver him over to us, and they delivered Joseph over to them, and they beheld him, that he was a very comely youth and they purchased him for twenty shekels.

(Jasher 44:3)
And the Ishmaelites continued their journey to Egypt and the Medanim also returned that day to Egypt, and the Medanim said to each other, Behold we have heard that Potiphar, an officer of Pharaoh, captain of the guard, seeks a good servant who shall stand before him to attend him, and to make him overseer over his house and all belonging to him.

(Jasher 44:4)
Now therefore come let us sell him to him for what we may desire, if he be able to give to us that which we shall require for him.

(Jasher 44:5)
And these Medanim went and came to the house of Potiphar, and said to him, We have heard that you seeks a good servant to attend you, behold we have a servant that will please you, if you can give to us that which we may desire, and we will sell him to you.

(Jasher 44:6)
And Potiphar said, Bring him before me, and I will see him, and if he please me I will give to you that which you may require for him.

(Jasher 44:7)
And the Medanim went and brought Joseph and placed him before Potiphar, and he saw him, and he pleased him exceedingly, and Potiphar said to them, Tell me what you require for this youth?

(Jasher 44:8)
And they said, Four hundred pieces of silver we desire for him, and Potiphar said, I will give it you if you bring me the record of his sale to you, and will tell me his history, for perhaps he may be stolen, for this youth is neither a slave, nor the son of a slave, but I observe in him the appearance of a goodly and handsome person.

(Jasher 44:9)
And the Medanim went and brought to him the Ishmaelites who had sold him to them, and they told him, saying, He is a slave and we sold him to them.

(Genesis 37:36) (Jasher 44:10) (...Jubilees 34:11)
And Potiphar heard the words of the Ishmaelites in his giving the silver to the Medanim, the Midianites therefore sold him into Egypt to Potiphar, an officer of Pharaoh's, and captain of the guard, the eunuch of Pharaoh, the chief of the cooks, priest of the city of Elew. And the Medanim took the silver and went on their journey, and the Ishmaelites also returned home.

Genesis: Chapter Thirty-Eight

(Jasher 45:1...) (Jubilees 34:20...)
And after Joseph perished, it was at that time in that year, which is the year of Joseph's going down to Egypt after his brothers had sold him, the sons of Jacob took to themselves wives.

(...Jasher 45:1) (...Jubilees 34:20...)
Reuben the son of Jacob went to Timnah and took to him for a wife Eliuram, the daughter of Avi the Canaanite, and he came to her.

(Jasher 45:2...)
And Eliuram the wife of Reuben conceived and bare him Hanoch, Palu, Chetzron and Carmi, four sons;

(...Jasher 45:2)
And Simeon his brother took his sister Dinah for a wife, and she bare to him Memuel, Yamin, Ohad, Jachin and Zochar, five sons.

(Jasher 45:3) (...Jubilees 34:20...)
And he afterward came to Bunah, the Canaanite woman, the same is Bunah whom Simeon took captive from the city of Shechem, and Bunah was before Dinah and attended upon her, and Simeon came to her, and she bare to him Saul.

(Jubilees 34:21)
And Simeon repented, and took a second wife from Mesopotamia as his brothers.

(Jasher 45:5, 6...)
And Levi and Issachar went to the land of the east, and they took to themselves for wives the daughters of Aram, of the seed of the sons of Terah of Jobab the son of Yoktan, the son of Eber; and Jobab the son of Yoktan had two daughters; the name of the elder was Adinah, and the name of the younger was Aridah.

(...Jasher 45:6...) (...Jubilees 34:20...)
And Levi took Adinah and Issachar took Aridah, and they came to the land of Canaan, to their father's house.

(...Jasher 45:6)
And Adinah bare to Levi, Gershon, Kehath and Merari; three sons.

(Jasher 45:7...)
And Aridah bare to Issachar Tola, Puvah, Job and Shomron, four sons;

(...Jasher 45:7) (...Jubilees 34:20...)
And Dan went to the land of Moab and took for a wife Aphlaleth, the daughter of Chamudan the Moabite, and he brought her to the land of Canaan.

(Jasher 45:8)
And Aphlaleth was barren, she had no offspring, and God afterward remembered Aphlaleth the wife of Dan, and she conceived and bare a son, and she called his name Chushim.

(Jasher 45:9)
And Gad and Naphtali went to Haran and took from thence the daughters of Amuram the son of Uz, the son of Nahor, for wives.

(Jasher 45:10) (...Jubilees 34:20...)
And these are the names of the daughters of Amuram; the name of the elder was Merimah, and the name of the younger Uzith; and Naphtali took Merimah of Mesopotamia; and Gad took Uzith; and brought them to the land of Canaan, to their father's house.

(Jasher 45:11)
And Merimah bare to Naphtali Yachzeel, Guni, Jazer and Shalem, four sons; and Uzith bare to Gad Zephion, Chagi, Shuni, Ezbon, Eri, Arodi and Arali, seven sons.

(Jasher 45:12) (...Jubilees 34:20...)
And Asher went forth and took Adon the daughter of Aphlal, the son of Hadad, the son of Ishmael, for a wife, and he brought her to the land of Canaan.

(Jasher 45:13)
And Adon the wife of Asher died in those days: she had no offspring; and it was after the death of Adon that Asher went to the other side of the river and took for a wife Hadurah the daughter of Abimael, the son of Eber, the son of Shem.

(Jasher 45:14)
And the young woman was of a comely appearance, and a woman of sense, and she had been the wife of Malkiel the son of Elam, the son of Shem.

(Jasher 45:15)
And Hadurah bare a daughter to Malkiel, and he called her name Serach, and Malkiel died after this, and Hadurah went and remained in her father's house.

(Jasher 45:16)
And after the death of the wife at Asher he went and took Hadurah for a wife, and brought her to the land of Canaan, and Serach her daughter he also brought with them, and she was three years old, and the damsel was brought up in Jacob's house.

(Jasher 45:17)
And the damsel was of a comely appearance, and she went in the sanctified ways of the children of Jacob; she lacked nothing, and the Lord gave her wisdom and understanding.

(Jasher 45:18)
And Hadurah the wife of Asher conceived and bare to him Yimnah, Yishvah, Yishvi and Beriah; four sons.

(Jasher 45:19)
And Zebulun went to Midian, and took for a wife Merishah the daughter of Molad, the son of Abida, the son of Midian, and brought her to the land of Canaan.

(Jasher 45:20)
And Merushah bare to Zebulun Sered, Elon and Yachleel; three sons.

(Jasher 45:21)
And Jacob sent to Aram, the son of Zoba, the son of Terah, and he took for his son Benjamin Mechalia the daughter of Aram, and she came to the land of Canaan to the house of Jacob; and Benjamin was ten years old when he took Mechalia the daughter of Aram for a wife.

(Jasher 45:22) (...Jubilees 34:20...)
And Mechalia conceived and bare to Benjamin Bela, Becher,

Ashbel, Gera and Naaman, five sons; and Benjamin went afterward and took for a wife Aribath, the daughter of Shomron, the son of Abraham, in addition to his first wife, and he was eighteen years old; and Aribath bare to Benjamin Achi, Vosh, Mupim, Chupim, and Ord; five sons.

(Genesis 38:1) (Jasher 45:4...)
And it came to pass at that time, that Judah went down from his brothers to Adulam, and turned in to a certain Adullamite, whose name was Hirah.

(Genesis 38:2) (...Jasher 45:4...) (...Jubilees 34:20...)
And Judah saw there a daughter of a certain Canaanite, whose name was Aliyath, the daughter of Shuah; and he took her, and went in to her.

(Genesis 38:3) (...Jasher 45:4...)
And Aliyath conceived, and bore a son to Judah; and he called his name Er.

(Genesis 38:4) (...Jasher 45:4...)
And Aliyath conceived again, and bore a son to Judah; and she called his name Onan.

(Genesis 38:5) (...Jasher 45:4)
And Aliyath yet again conceived, and bore a son to Judah; and called his name Shelah: and he was at Chezib, when she bore him.

(Genesis 38:6) (Jasher 45:23) (Jubilees 41:1)
And in those days, in the forty-fifth jubilee, in the second week, in the second year, Judah went to the house of Shem and took a wife for Er his firstborn, from the daughters of Aram, whose name was Tamar, the daughter of Elam, the son of Shem.

(Jubilees 41:2)
But he hated, and did not lie with her, because his mother was of the daughters of Canaan, and he wished to take him a wife of the kinsfolk of his mother, but Judah, his father, would not permit him.

(Genesis 38:7) (Jasher 45:24) (Jubilees 41:3)
And Er, Judah's firstborn, came to his wife Tamar, and she became his wife, and when he came to her he outwardly destroyed his seed, and his work was wicked in the sight of the LORD; and the LORD slew him.

(Genesis 38:8) (Jasher 45:25) (Jubilees 41:4)
And it was after the death of Er, Judah's first born, that Judah said to Onan, his brother: Go in to your brother's wife, and marry her as the next of kin, and perform the duty of a husband's brother to her, and raise up seed to your brother.

(Genesis 38:9) (Jasher 45:26...) (Jubilees 41:5...)
And Onan took Tamar for a wife. And Onan knew that the seed would not be his (but) his brother's only; and it came to pass, when he went in to the house of his brother's wife, and Onan also did like to the work of his brother, and he spilled the seed on the ground, lest that he should give seed to his brother.

(Genesis 38:10) (...Jasher 45:26) (...Jubilees 41:5)
And the thing which he did displeased the LORD: and he slew him also.

(Genesis 38:11) (Jasher 45:27, 28) (Jubilees 41:6)
Then when Onan died, Judah said to Tamar his daughter in law, Remain a widow at your father's house, till Shelah my son is grown and I shall give you to him to wife. And Judah

delighted no more in Tamar, to give her to Shiloh, for he said, Lest peradventure he die also, as his brothers did. And Tamar rose up and went and dwelt in her father's house. And Tamar was in her father's house for some time.

(Genesis 38:12) (Jasher 45:29) (Jubilees 41:7, 8...)
And in process of time, Shelah grew up; but Bedsu'el, the wife of Judah, did not permit her son Shelah to marry. And at the revolution of the year, Aliyath, the daughter of Shuah, Judah's wife died, in the fifth year of this week; and Judah was comforted for his wife, and in the sixth year after the death of Aliyath, Judah went up to his sheep shearers to Timnath, he and his friend Hirah the Adullamite.

(Genesis 38:13) (Jasher 45:30...) (...Jubilees 41:8)
And it was told Tamar, saying, Behold, your father-in-law goes up to Timnath to shear his sheep.

(Genesis 38:14) (...Jasher 45:30, 31) (Jubilees 41:9)
And Tamar rose up and she put her widow's garments off from her, and covered her with a veil, and adorned herself, and wrapped herself and she entirely covered herself, and sat in an open place in the gate which is by the way to Timnath; for she saw that Shelah was grown, and Judah did not delight in her and she was not given to him to wife.

(Genesis 38:15) (Jasher 45:32...) (Jubilees 41:10...)
When Judah passed and saw her, he thought her to be a harlot; because she had covered her face.

(Genesis 38:16) (...Jubilees 41:10, 11...)
And he turned to her by the way, and he said to her, Go to, I pray, let me come in to you; (for he did not know that she was his daughter in law.) And she said to him: Come in, and he

went in. And she said to him: What will you give me, that you may come in to me? Give me my hire.

(Genesis 38:17) (Jubilees 41:12...)
And he said I will send you a kid from the flock. And she said, Will you give me a pledge, till you send it?

(Genesis 38:18) (...Jasher 45:32...) (...Jubilees 41:11, ...12)
And he said to her: I have nothing in my hand save my ring that is on my finger, and my necklace, and my staff which is in my hand. What pledge shall I give you? And she said to him, Your signet, and your bracelets, and your staff that is in your hand, Give them to me until you send me my hire. And he gave it her, and took her, and came in to her, and she conceived by him.

(Genesis 38:19) (Jubilees 41:13)
And Judah went to his sheep, and she arose, and went away to her father's house, and laid by her veil from her, and put on the garments of her widowhood.

(Genesis 38:20) (Jubilees 41:14...)
And Judah sent the kid of the goats by the hand of his shepherd friend the Adullamite, to receive his pledge from the woman's hand: but he couldn't find her.

(Genesis 38:21) (...Jubilees 41:14)
Then he asked the men of that place, saying, Where is the harlot, that was here openly by the way side? And they said, There was no harlot here with us in this place.

(Genesis 38:22) (Jubilees 41:15)
And he returned to Judah, and informed him and said to him,

I cannot find her; and also, I asked the men of the place, and they said, that there was no harlot here in this place.

(Genesis 38:23) (Jubilees 41:16...)
And Judah said, Let her take it to her, lest we be shamed, a cause of derision: behold, I sent this kid, and you have not found her.

(Genesis 38:24) (...Jubilees 41:16, 17)
And it came to pass about three months after, that it was manifest that she was with child, and they told Judah, saying, Tamar your daughter in law has played the harlot; and also, behold, she is with child by whoredom. And Judah went to the house of her father, and said to her father and her brothers: Bring her forth, and let her be burnt, for she has wrought uncleanness in Israel.

(Genesis 38:25) (Jubilees 41:18)
And it came to pass when she was brought forth to burn her, she sent to her father-in-law the ring and the necklace, and the staff, saying, By the man who these belong to, I am with child: and she said, Discern, I pray, whose are these, the signet, and bracelets, and staff.

(Genesis 38:26) (Jubilees 41:19, 20)
And Judah acknowledged them, and said, She has been more righteous than I; because that I gave her not to Shelah my son. And therefore, let them burn her not. And for that reason, she was not given to Shelah, And he knew her again no more.

(Genesis 38:27) (...Jasher 45:32...)
And it came to pass in the time of her travail, that, behold, twins were in her womb.

(Genesis 38:28)

And it came to pass, when she travailed, that the one put out his hand: and the midwife took and bound on his hand a scarlet thread, saying, This came out first.

(Genesis 38:29) (...Jasher 45:32)

And it came to pass, as he drew back his hand, that, behold, his brother came out: and she said, How have you broken forth? This breach be on you: therefore his name was called Pharez.

(Genesis 38:30)

And afterward came out his brother, that had the scarlet thread on his hand: and his name was called Zarah.

(Jubilees 41:21)

So Tamar bare two sons, Perez and Zerah, in the seventh year of this second week.

(Jubilees 41:22)

And thereupon the seven years of fruitfulness were accomplished, of which Joseph spoke to Pharaoh.

(Jubilees 41:23)

And Judah acknowledged that the deed which he had done was evil, for he had lain with his daughter-in-law, and he esteemed it hateful in his eyes, and he acknowledged that he had transgressed and gone astray, for he had uncovered the skirt of his son, and he began to lament and to supplicate before the Lord because of his transgression.

(Jubilees 41:24)

And we told him in a dream that he was forgiven because

he supplicated earnestly, and lamented, and did not again commit it.

(Jubilees 41:25)
And he received forgiveness because he turned from his sin and from his ignorance, for he transgressed greatly before our God; and everyone that acts thus, everyone who lies with his mother-in-law, let them burn him with fire that he may burn therein, for there is uncleanness and pollution on them, with fire let them burn them.

(Jubilees 41:26)
And do you command the children of Israel that there be no uncleanness amongst them, for everyone who lies with his daughter-in-law or with his mother-in-law has wrought uncleanness; with fire let them burn the man who has lain with her, and likewise the woman, and He will turn away wrath and punishment from Israel.

(Jubilees 41:27)
And to Judah we said that his two sons had not lain with her, and for this reason his seed was established for a second generation, and would not be rooted out.

(Jubilees 41:28)
For in singleness of eye he had gone and sought for punishment, namely, according to the judgment of Abraham, which he had commanded his sons, Judah had sought to burn her with fire.

Genesis: Chapter Thirty-Nine

(Jubilees 39:1)
And Jacob dwelt in the land of his father's sojournings in the land of Canaan. These are the generations of Jacob.

(Genesis 39:1) (Jubilees 39:2)
And Joseph was seventeen years old when they brought him down to the land of Egypt; and Potiphar, an officer of Pharaoh, captain of the guard, a eunuch of Pharaoh, the chief cook, an Egyptian, bought him of the hands of the Ishmaelites, which had brought him down there.

(Jasher 44:11...)
And Potiphar took Joseph and brought him to his house that he might serve him.

(Genesis 39:2) (Jasher 44:12...)
And the LORD was with Joseph, and he was a prosperous man; and he was in the house of his master the Egyptian.

(Genesis 39:3)
And his master saw that the LORD was with him, and that the LORD made all that he did to prosper in his hand.

(Genesis 39:4) (...Jasher 44:11) (Jubilees 39:3...)
And Joseph found grace in his sight, and he served him: and he placed confidence in him, and he made him overseer over his house, and all that he had he put into his hand.

(Genesis 39:5) (...Jasher 44:12) (...Jubilees 39:3)
And it came to pass from the time that he had made him overseer in his house, and over all that he had, that the LORD blessed the Egyptian's house for Joseph's sake; and the blessing of the LORD was on all that he had in the house, and in the field, and the Lord prospered him in all that he did.

(Genesis 39:6) (Jasher 44:13) (Jubilees 39:4)
And Potiphar the Egyptian left all that he had in Joseph's hand; for he saw that the Lord was with him, and that the Lord prospered him in all that he did. And Joseph was one that caused things to come in and go out, and everything was regulated by his wish in the house of Potiphar. And he did not know everything he had, save the bread which he ate. And Joseph was a goodly person, and well favored.

(Genesis 39:7...) (Jasher 44:14) (Jubilees 39:5...)
And Joseph was eighteen years old, a youth with beautiful eyes. And Joseph's appearance was comely and very beautiful was his appearance and like to him was not in the whole land of Egypt.

(...Genesis 39:7) (Jasher 44:15, 16) (...Jubilees 39:5)
And at that time while he was in his master's house, going in and out of the house and attending his master, it came to pass after these things, that Zelicah, his master's wife, cast her eyes on Joseph, and she looked at him, and behold he was a youth comely and well favored. And she coveted his beauty in her heart, and her soul was fixed upon Joseph, and she loved him and besought him to lie with her, and she said, Lay with me. And she enticed him day after day, and Zelicah persuaded Joseph daily, but Joseph did not lift up his eyes to behold his master's wife.

(Jasher 44:17)
And Zelicah said to him, How goodly are your appearance and form, truly I have looked at all the slaves, and have not seen so beautiful a slave as you are; and Joseph said to her, Surely he who created me in my mother's womb created all mankind.

(Jasher 44:18)
And she said to him, How beautiful are your eyes, with which you have dazzled all the inhabitants of Egypt, men and women; and he said to her, How beautiful they are while we are alive, but should you behold them in the grave, surely you would move away from them.

(Jasher 44:19)
And she said to him, How beautiful and pleasing are all your words; take now, I pray you, the harp which is in the house, and play with your hands and let us hear your words.

(Jasher 44:20)
And he said to her, How beautiful and pleasing are my words when I speak the praise of my God and his glory; and she said to him, How very beautiful is the hair of your head, behold the golden comb which is in the house, take it I pray you, and curl the hair of your head.

(Jasher 44:21)
And he said to her, How long will you speak these words? Cease to utter these words to me, and rise and attend to your domestic affairs.

(Jasher 44:22)
And she said to him, There is no one in my house, and there is nothing to attend to but to your words and to your wish; yet

notwithstanding all this, she could not bring Joseph to her, neither did he place his eye upon her, but directed his eyes below to the ground.

(Jasher 44:23)
And Zelicah desired Joseph in her heart, that he should lie with her, and at the time that Joseph was sitting in the house doing his work, Zelicah came and sat before him, and she enticed him daily with her discourse to lie with her, or ever to look at her, but Joseph would not hearken to her.

(Jasher 44:24)
And she said to him, If you will not do according to my words, I will chastise you with the punishment of death, and put an iron yoke upon you.

(Jasher 44:25)
And Joseph said to her, Surely God who created man lets loose the fetters of prisoners, and it is he who will deliver me from your prison and from your judgment.

(Jasher 44:26)
And when she could not prevail over him, to persuade him, and her soul being still fixed upon him, her desire threw her into a grievous sickness.

(Jasher 44:27)
And all the women of Egypt came to visit her, and they said to her, Why are you in this declining state? You that lack nothing; surely your husband is a great and esteemed prince in the sight of the king, should you lack anything of what your heart desires?

(Jasher 44:28)
And Zelicah answered them, saying, This day it shall be made known to you, from where this disorder springs in which you see me, and she commanded her maid servants to prepare food for all the women, and she made a banquet for them, and all the women ate in the house of Zelicah.

(Jasher 44:29)
And she gave them knives to peel the citrons to eat them, and she commanded that they should dress Joseph in costly garments, and that he should appear before them, and Joseph came before their eyes and all the women looked on Joseph, and could not take their eyes from off him, and they all cut their hands with the knives that they had in their hands, and all the citrons that were in their hands were filled with blood.

(Jasher 44:30)
And they knew not what they had done but they continued to look at the beauty of Joseph, and did not turn their eyelids from him.

(Jasher 44:31)
And Zelicah saw what they had done, and she said to them, What is this work that you have done? Behold I gave you citrons to eat and you have all cut your hands.

(Jasher 44:32)
And all the women saw their hands, and behold they were full of blood, and their blood flowed down upon their garments, and they said to her, this slave in your house has overcome us, and we could not turn our eyelids from him on account of his beauty.

(Jasher 44:33)
And she said to them, Surely this happened to you in the moment that you looked at him, and you could not contain yourselves from him; how then can I refrain when he is constantly in my house, and I see him day after day going in and out of my house? How then can I keep from declining or even from perishing on account of this?

(Jasher 44:34)
And they said to her, the words are true, for who can see this beautiful form in the house and refrain from him, and is he not your slave and attendant in your house, and why do you not tell him that which is in your heart, and suffer your soul to perish through this matter?

(Jasher 44:35)
And she said to them, I am daily endeavoring to persuade him, and he will not consent to my wishes, and I promised him everything that is good, and yet I could meet with no return from him; I am therefore in a declining state as you see.

(Jasher 44:36)
And Zelicah became very ill on account of her desire toward Joseph, and she was desperately lovesick on account of him, and all the people of the house of Zelicah and her husband knew nothing of this matter, that Zelicah was ill on account of her love to Joseph.

(Jasher 44:37)
And all the people of her house asked her, saying, Why are you ill and declining, and lack nothing? And she said to them, I know not this thing which is daily increasing upon me.

(Jasher 44:38)
And all the women and her friends came daily to see her, and they spoke with her, and she said to them, This can only be through the love of Joseph; and they said to her, Entice him and seize him secretly, perhaps he may hearken to you, and put off this death from you.

(Jasher 44:39)
And Zelicah became worse from her love to Joseph, and she continued to decline, till she had scarce strength to stand.

(Jasher 44:40)
And on a certain day Joseph was doing his master's work in the house, and Zelicah came secretly and fell suddenly upon him, and Joseph rose up against her, and he was more powerful than she, and he brought her down to the ground.

(Jasher 44:41)
And Zelicah wept on account of the desire of her heart toward him, and she supplicated him with weeping, and her tears flowed down her cheeks, and she spoke to him in a voice of supplication and in bitterness of soul, saying,

(Jasher 44:42)
Have you ever heard, seen or known of so beautiful a woman as I am, or better than myself, who speak daily to you, fall into a decline through love for you, confer all this honor upon you, and still you will not hearken to my voice?

(Jasher 44:43)
And if it be through fear of your master lest he punish you, as the king lives no harm shall come to you from your master through this thing; now, therefore pray listen to me, and consent for the sake of the honor which I have conferred upon

you, and put off this death from me, and why should I die for your sake? And she ceased to speak.

(Jubilees 39:6)
But he did not surrender his soul, and he remembered the Lord and the words which Jacob, his father, used to read from among the words of Abraham, that no man should commit fornication with a woman who has a husband; that for him the punishment of death has been ordained in the heavens before the Most High God, and the sin will be recorded against him in the eternal books continually before the Lord.

(Genesis 39:8) (Jasher 44:44) (Jubilees 39:7)
But Joseph remembered these words and he refused to lie with her. And Joseph answered and said to his master's wife, Refrain from me, and leave this matter to my master; Behold, my master does not worry about what is with me in the house, and he has committed all that he has to my hand, and how shall I do these things in my master's house?

(Genesis 39:9) (Jasher 44:45)
For he hath also greatly honored me in his house, and he hath also made me overseer over his house, and he hath exalted me, and there is none greater in this house than I; neither has he kept back anything from me but you, because you are his wife: how then can you speak these words to me, and how then can I do this great wickedness, and sin against God and to your husband?

(Jasher 44:46)
Now therefore refrain from me, and speak no more such words as these, for I will not hearken to your words. But Zelicah would not hearken to Joseph when he spoke these words to her, but she daily enticed him to listen to her.

(Genesis 39:10) (Jubilees 39:8)

And it came to pass, she spoke to Joseph day by day for a year, but he refused and he did not hearken to her, to lay by her, or to be with her.

(Jasher 44:47)

And it was after this that the brook of Egypt was filled above all its sides, and all the inhabitants of Egypt went forth, and also the king and princes went forth with timbrels and dances, for it was a great rejoicing in Egypt, and a holiday at the time of the inundation of the sea Sihor, and they went there to rejoice all the day.

(Jasher 44:48)

And when the Egyptians went out to the river to rejoice, as was their custom, all the people of the house of Potiphar went with them, but Zelicah would not go with them, for she said, I am indisposed, and she remained alone in the house, and no other person was with her in the house.

(Jasher 44:49...)

And she rose up and ascended to her temple in the house, and dressed herself in princely garments, and she placed upon her head precious stones of onyx stones, inlaid with silver and gold, and she beautified her face and skin with all sorts of women's purifying liquids, and she perfumed the temple and the house with cassia and frankincense, and she spread myrrh and aloes, and she afterward sat in the entrance of the temple, in the passage of the house, through which Joseph passed to do his work,

(Genesis 39:11) (...Jasher 44:49)

And it came to pass about this time, that behold Joseph came from the field, and went into the house to do his master's business; and there were none of the men of the house inside.

(Jasher 44:50)
And he came to the place through which he had to pass, and he saw all the work of Zelicah, and he turned back.

(Jasher 44:51)
And Zelicah saw Joseph turning back from her, and she called out to him, saying What ails you Joseph? Come to your work, and behold I will make room for you until you shall have passed to your seat.

(Jasher 44:52)
And Joseph returned and came to the house, and passed from thence to the place of his seat, and he sat down to do his master's work as usual and behold Zelicah came to him and stood before him in princely garments, and the scent from her clothes was spread to a distance.

(Genesis 39:12...) (Jasher 44:53) (Jubilees 39:9...)
And she hastened and caught him by his garment, embraced him and held him fast in the house in order to force him to lie with her, and closed the doors of the house and held him fast; saying, Lay with me: and she said to him, As the king lives if you will not perform my request you shall die this day, and she hastened and stretched forth her other hand and drew a sword from beneath her garments, and she placed it upon Joseph's neck, and she said, Rise and perform my request, and if not, you will die this day.

(...Genesis 39:12) (Jasher 44:54) (...Jubilees 39:9)
And Joseph was afraid of her at her doing this thing, and he rose up to flee from her, and she seized the front of his garments, and in the terror of his flight the garment which Zelicah seized was torn, and he left his garment in her hand and broke through the door, and fled, and got himself out from her presence, for he was in fear.

(Genesis 39:13) (Jasher 44:55) (Jubilees 39:10...)

And it came to pass, the woman saw that he would not lie with her. And when she saw that Joseph's garment was torn, and that he had left his garment in her hand, and was fled forth, she was afraid of her life, lest the report should spread concerning her, and she rose up and acted with cunning, and put off the garments in which she was dressed, and she put on her other garments.

(Jasher 44:56...)

And she took Joseph's garment, and she laid it beside her, and she went and seated herself in the place where she had sat in her illness, before the people of her house had gone out to the river.

(Genesis 39:14) (...Jasher 44:56, 57)

That she called a young lad who was then in the house, and she ordered him to the men of her house. And when she saw them she spoke to them with a loud voice and lamentation, saying, See, he has brought in an Hebrew to us in the house, to mock us; he came in to me to lay with me, and I cried with a loud voice:

(Jasher 44:58)

For when you had gone out he came to the house, and seeing that there was no person in the house, he came to me, and caught hold of me, with intent to lie with me.

(Genesis 39:15) (Jasher 44:59)

And I seized his garments and tore them and called out against him with a loud voice, and it came to pass, when he heard that I lifted up my voice and cried, that he was afraid of his life and he left his garment with me, and fled, and got himself out.

(Jasher 44:60)
And the people of her house spoke nothing, but their wrath was very much kindled against Joseph, and they went to his master and told him the words of his wile.

(Genesis 39:16)
And she laid up his garment by her, until his lord came home.

(Genesis 39:17) (Jasher 44:61) (...Jubilees 39:10...)
And Potiphar came home enraged, and his wife cried out to him, and she spoke to him, and she calumniated Joseph in the presence of his lord, according to these words, saying, What is this thing that you have done, the Hebrew servant, whom you love, which you have brought to us, into my house, came in to me to mock me, he sought to force me so that he might lie with me; thus he did to me this day.

(Genesis 39:18) (...Jubilees 39:10)
And it came to pass, as I lifted up my voice and cried, that when I held him, he left his garment with me in my hands, and he broke through the door, and fled out.

(Genesis 39:19) (Jubilees 39:11...)
And it came to pass, when his master the Egyptian saw the garment of Joseph and the broken door, and heard the words of his wife, which she spoke to him, saying, After this manner, your servant did to me; that his wrath was kindled.

(Jasher 44:62)
And Potiphar heard the words of his wife, and he ordered Joseph to be punished with severe stripes, and they did so to him.

(Jasher 44:63)
And while they were smiting him, Joseph called out with a loud voice, and he lifted up his eyes to heaven, and he said, O Lord God, you know that I am innocent of all these things, and why shall I die this day through falsehood, by the hand of these uncircumcised wicked men, whom you know?

(Jasher 44:64)
And while Potiphar's men were beating Joseph, he continued to cry out and weep, and there was a child there eleven months old, and the Lord opened the mouth of the child, and he spoke these words before Potiphar's men, who were smiting Joseph, saying,

(Jasher 44:65)
What do you want of this man, and why do you do this evil to him? My mother speaks falsely and utter lies; thus was the transaction.

(Jasher 44:66)
And the child told them accurately all that happened, and all the words of Zelicah to Joseph day after day he declared to them.

(Jasher 44:67)
And all the men heard the words of the child and they wondered greatly at the child's words, and the child ceased to speak and became still.

(Jasher 44:68)
And Potiphar was very much ashamed at the words of his son, and he commanded his men not to beat Joseph any more, and the men ceased beating Joseph.

(Jasher 44:69)
And Potiphar took Joseph and ordered him to be brought to justice before the priests, who were judges belonging to the king, in order to judge him concerning this affair.

(Jasher 44:70)
And Potiphar and Joseph came before the priests who were the king's judges, and he said to them, Decide I pray you, what judgment is due to a servant, for thus has he done.

(Jasher 44:71)
And the priests said to Joseph, Why did you do this thing to your master? And Joseph answered them, saying, Not so my lords, thus was the matter; and Potiphar said to Joseph, Surely I entrusted in your hands all that belonged to me, and I withheld nothing from you but my wife, and how could you do this evil?

(Jasher 44:72)
And Joseph answered saying, Not so my lord, as the Lord lives, and as your soul lives, my lord, the word which you heard from your wife is untrue, for thus was the affair this day.

(Jasher 44:73)
A year has elapsed to me since I have been in your house; have you seen any iniquity in me, or anything which might cause you to demand my life?

(Jasher 44:74)
And the priests said to Potiphar, Send, we pray you, and let them bring before us Joseph's torn garment, and let us see the tear in it, and if it shall be that the tear is in front of the garment, then his face must have been opposite to her and

she must have caught hold of him, to come to her, and with deceit did your wife do all that she has spoken.

(Jasher 44:75)
And they brought Joseph's garment before the priests who were judges, and they saw and behold the tear was in front of Joseph, and all the judging priests knew that she had pressed him, and they said, The judgment of death is not due to this slave for he has done nothing, but his judgment is, that he be placed in the prison house on account of the report, which through him has gone forth against your wife.

(Genesis 39:20) (Jasher 44:76...) (...Jubilees 39:11, 12...)
And Potiphar, Joseph's master, heard their words, and he took him, and put him into the prison, a place where the king's prisoners were bound: and he was there in the prison.

(Genesis 39:21) (...Jubilees 39:12...)
But the LORD was with Joseph, and showed him mercy, and gave him favor in the sight of the keeper of the prison, the chief of the prison guards and compassion before him.

(Genesis 39:22) (Jubilees 39:13...)
And the keeper of the prison committed to Joseph's hand all the prisoners that were in the prison; and whatsoever they did there, he did; he committed all things into his hands. For Joseph did everything, and the Lord perfected it.

(Genesis 39:23) (...Jubilees 39:12, ...13)
The keeper of the prison looked not to anything that was under his hand; because he saw that the LORD was with him, and that which he did, the LORD made it to prosper.

Epilogue

(...Jasher 44:76)
And Joseph was in the house of confinement twelve years.

(Jasher 44:77)
And notwithstanding this, his master's wife did not turn from him, and she did not cease from speaking to him day after day to hearken to her, and at the end of three months Zelicah continued going to Joseph to the house of confinement day by day, and she enticed him to hearken to her, and Zelicah said to Joseph, How long will you remain in this house? But hearken now to my voice, and I will bring you out of this house.

(Jasher 44:78)
And Joseph answered her, saying, It is better for me to remain in this house than to hearken to your words, to sin against God; and she said to him, If you will not perform my wish, I will pluck out your eyes, add fetters to your feet, and will deliver you into the hands of them whom you did not know before.

(Jasher 44:79)
And Joseph answered her and said, Behold the God of the whole earth is able to deliver me from all that you can do to me, for he opens the eyes of the blind, and lets loose those that are bound, and preserves all strangers who are unacquainted with the land.

(Jasher 44:80)
And when Zelicah was unable to persuade Joseph to hearken to her, she left off going to entice him; and Joseph was still confined in the house of confinement. And Jacob the father of Joseph, and all his brothers who were in the land of Canaan still mourned and wept in those days on account of Joseph, for Jacob refused to be comforted for his son Joseph, and Jacob cried aloud, and wept and mourned all those days.

Final Notes

We hope your journey is enriched and you are blessed through the production of the **Ancient Texts and the Bible** series!

Minister 2 Others would like to hear from you. If you have comments or questions concerning our materials, or if you find errors in our projects, misspellings, or formatting issues. We work hard to provide quality materials, however, sometimes things can squeak by unnoticed. Your feedback is truly appreciated.

We love producing helpful, innovative books and we are grateful for your support! If you have enjoyed this production, please consider writing a review and letting others know about our materials.

If you would like to be updated when we release new books and other materials, please sign up for our e-newsletter on our website.

Thanks!

Minister 2 Others

Minister2others.com

www.ingramcontent.com/pod-product-compliance
Lightning Source LLC
Chambersburg PA
CBHW071257190726
48292CB00007B/2572

* 9 7 8 1 9 4 7 7 5 1 2 2 4 *